ALEXANDER DOLLS
Collector's Price Guide
by A. Glenn Mandeville

Published by **Hobby House Press, Inc.**
Grantsville, MD 21536

Hobby House Press

Dedication

This second edition of Alexander Dolls Value Guide is dedicated to Daun Fallon, and Therese J. Stadelmeier, the two head designers at the Alexander Doll Company. It is a rare thing today to see talent based on a respect for the past, coupled with the technology of today, and a vision of the future. In addition to indisputible talent, these young ladies make themselves available at collectors events to assist in any way they can to make your collecting more enjoyable. They truly are carrying on the traditions that made the Alexander Doll Company what it is today.

Acknowledgements

After the first edition of *Alexander Dolls Value Guide* was published, many individuals came forth with choice information that makes this new, revised edition worthy of your attention, they are: Jan Lebow, Marge and Earl Meisinger, Bernice Heister, Jean Bartenfeld, Jay Schwartz of Julius Levinson, Inc., Benita Schwartz, and Chris Law. The following, whose help launched the first edition, is still greatly appreciated, they are: Joe Carillo, Vivian Brady-Ashley, Ann Tardie, Pat Burns, Ann Rast, Neal Foster, Tanya McWhorter, and Ira Smith, CEO of The Alexander Doll Company. The author would especially like to acknowledge the research on dates by Judy Traina and Linda Collie, and the editorial fine tuning by Mary Beth Ruddell of Hobby House Press, Inc. I am personally indebted to Marge and Earl Mesinger and Pamela Martinec for providing photographs of their Alexander Doll Collections. Also, the late Bob Gantz contributed more to this book than could ever be listed. Without these individuals, I could not have successfully undertaken such a large project. Many, many thanks.

FRONT COVER: This mint 14in (36cm) *Margaret O'Brien* doll is complete with her clover wrist tag. She is all composition and dates from the mid 1940s. *A. Glenn Mandeville Collection.*

TITLE PAGE: This stunning 21in (53cm) *Cissy Bride*, 1921 was the one-of-a-kind auction piece for the 1993 Walt Disney World® Teddy Bear and Doll Convention. *Chris Law Collection. Photograph courtesy of Chris Law.*

Additional copies of this book may be purchased at $11.95 (plus postage and handling) from

Hobby House Press, Inc.

1 Corporate Drive
Grantsville, Maryland 21536
1-800-554-1447
or from your favorite bookstore or dealer.

Table of Contents

For four straight years in the early 1950s Madame Alexander won the prestigious Fashion Academy Award for Clothing Design. She is shown here in her office with three of her award-winning designs. *A. Glenn Mandeville Collection.*

The Magic of Collecting Madame Alexander Dolls

There is indeed much magic, that elusive mystery and wonderment, that comes from just looking at a Madame Alexander doll. In my opinion, no other doll can come close to the quality, workmanship and theme selections of the creations produced for over seventy years at The Alexander Doll Company.

During the "Golden Age" of the collectible dolls, namely the late 1940s until the mid 1960s, Madame Alexander dolls were the standard by which all other dolls were judged. It matters little if Madame was first with a new idea. When she entered the race, her version was always the best. Although Madame Alexander dolls cost much more than competitors' dolls, it was the quality and exquisite design that made Madame Alexander a legend.

The most overlooked fact is that Madame was not a doll artist but a clothing designer. She won the Fashion Academy Award for clothing design four straight years, 1951-1954. More astonishing is that the competition was not just doll clothing but ALL garment manufactured, period. This was and still is, a large part of the magic of Madame Alexander dolls. Each perfectly tailored little garment could be made for a miniature person. If you were only eight inches tall, you had an entire playground realm - ball gowns, street wear, play clothes and more in your imaginary closet!

The dolls were rarely the stars because at The Alexander Doll Company the tradition is to take a face and use it to launch a thousand ships. To Madame, the dolls, for the most part, were merely the mannequins upon which she draped her dreams and her desire to educate those who would possess her creations.

Expensive and only available in "better" outlets, the dolls Madame created embodied her belief that today's child was underexposed to the great masters of art, literature and culture. It was through her dolls, the notables such as *Morisot, Renoir, Mary Cassatt*, that others became familiar with their histories.

A life of culture, often neglected even in the educated, became real as the same little 12" (31cm) doll became Lord Fauntleroy, Napolean and Josephine, Anthony and Cleopatra, and even Rhett and Scarlett! One doll, one face, yet in the skillful hands of The Alexander Doll Company, magic WAS created as each new character came to life.

There is magic in collecting Madame Alexander dolls. For over 70 years, Madame Alexander and The Alexander Doll Company, are providing us with a history and art that thrill to amaze us. They are proving that a thing of beauty is truly a joy forever.

A 1966 *Scarlett* Portrait doll. Using the same mold as the *Coco* doll from that year, this *Scarlett* is the most valuable and magical of all the Portrait dolls. The *Coco* doll is regarded as the jewel in the crown of Madame Alexander dolls. *A. Glenn Mandeville Collection.*

What IS My Alexander Doll Worth?

As a collector and appraiser of dolls, the most frequent question I am asked, when at shows or by mail, is what is my Alexander doll worth?

The question, while seemingly simple can be compared to asking a stranger you meet "What is my car worth?" The person hearing the question would be shocked, as no further information is often given!

Some basic facts must be discussed. Antique dolls, defined as having a porcelain head and over 75 years old, are evaluated quite differently than Madame Alexander dolls.

With an antique doll, the value is primarily in the head of the doll. The mold number, and the facial expression can add up to a doll head that is worth tens of thousands of dollars. The body can usually be "replaced" at a later date. "Period" clothing can always be found at a good doll show if it is missing but basically, the assigned value of the doll is contained from the neck up!

Madame Alexander dolls are another matter entirely; first, each doll is almost without exception, like hundreds, even thousands of others. What makes the doll unique is the clothing, the wig, and the face painting. Thus a nude, wigless, Alexander doll has little, if any value, because the character of the doll is lost forever. Is it *Little Miss Muffet*, or maybe *Oliver Twist*? Could the nude, wigless little creature be a boy or a girl? An adult or a child?

The reader can quickly see that to bring top collector dollars, the doll must be complete with all the original accessories it was sold with.

Secondly, the condition of the doll is almost all the value. The same collectors that stared lovingly at the doll cases in John Wanamaker's in Philadelphia want that doll to look just as it did in 1957! After all, they remember it that way and waited over thirty years to own it! Certainly they are not interested in used children's toys. They want, and are willing to pay for, per-fection. The collector wants to cheat time, as it were, and pretend that it is Christmas morning, 1957, and they are opening the dream doll they never received!

With Alexander dolls, the seller must realize the further you take the doll from crispy mint perfection, the lower the price goes. One has to understand that even with very rare dolls, the doll is either unplayed with and in mint condition, or it falls into the category of a used child's toy. Naturally, the played with doll has some value, often more sentimental than monetary, but the price drops drastically along with condition.

Factors which add to the value of an Alexander doll are: Does the doll have original factory clothing, complete with all accessories? Is there a box? Does the doll have a booklet or wrist tag? Also factors such as a good facial coloring and general eye appeal make for a superior doll.

There is much misunderstanding in the pricing of Alexander dolls. Some collectors will buy gently played with dolls and restore them, but they want the price to reflect the effort that they have to put forth to bring the doll up to another level. Other collectors simply will not look at a pale, badly played with doll and regard it as something that should be discarded or purchased for parts.

Sellers of dolls are becoming more educated to the fact that condition is the main ingredient in making an Alexander doll valuable. The dealer of today is more often a collector him/herself and thus very in tune to the factors that make an Alexander doll valuable.

Another question that I am often asked "How do I keep my collection from overtaking my house?" Many times a doll collector, myself included, loves EVERY-THING. Naturally, if space and money were not a consideration, I suppose this would not be a problem, but I can offer the collector my favorite ten tips to make your collection award winning!

The prize of anyone's collection would be this stunning all composition *Jane Withers*. Complete with gold plated signature pin, she was made from a special doll mold. Her like new condition makes her a star! *A. Glenn Mandeville Collection.*

Ten Tips to Make Your Collection Award Winning!

1. Decide on a focus for your collection. Stick to one particular size doll, or perhaps a theme such as fairy tale characters. By sticking to a category you can avoid the "I have to have everything they make" anxiety and strengthen your collection. What happens if you see an Alexander doll that is NOT in your category but you MUST have? Well, like the person on a diet, you can splurge on that hot fudge sundae a few times, but not everyday!

2. Buy the best you can afford and don't be afraid to upgrade if you see a better example. This is one area where you CAN be a bit obsessive! With older dolls, ask yourself if this doll is a better example than the one you have at home. Sometimes new dolls have fabric varia-

tions. If you see one you like better, buy it and sell yours. The goal is always to have a strong collection in your chosen category.

3. If you are collecting a series, such as Americana dolls or foreign lands figures or anything similar, carry a small notebook with you to doll shows.That way you will remember what it is you need to complete a certain grouping.

4. Always note what accessories you need to make a doll go up a grade. Your notebook can list things like booklets, wrist tags, shoes, stockings, hats, etc., that can make a doll go from excellent to mint condition.It is possible to find these little things, I speak from experience, so note what it is you need.

5. Money is usually a factor with most collectors. If you see a doll at a show you need, inquire if the dealer has a lay-a-way policy. Credit cards (a necessary evil in collecting) can be an option. When all else fails, at least get the name and phone number of the seller. Some dealers do only a couple of shows a year and it IS possible that the item you are interested in will be available when you have the funds!

6. Assign each doll a code number. I use a letter code for the year and a number code for the item within that year. In other words, if 1993 is "A" and your first item is "1" this makes your code "A-1". Use a small self-stick label to put your code on the bottom of the doll's shoe. In a notebook record: the date of purchase, check number, receipt from the seller, etc. Insure your collection and photograph your dolls. Keep this information in duplicate in a place off the premises such as a safe deposit box or at a family member's home.

7. Enjoy your collection by taking the dolls out of the boxes. Rotate a display around a holiday theme or family tradition. Invest in built-in cabinets or curio cases. Having a doll out in the air for a month or so will not hurt it and will give the material a chance to "breathe" Remember, there are only a few precautions you need to follow: keep dolls out of direct sunlight or even brightly lit areas; avoid dust by using cases; and keep dolls away from small children and pets. I think it is better to risk a little wear and tear on your treasures, then have them all packed away.

8. Read all you can on Alexander dolls. There are many excellent publications that can assist you. Company catalogs are invaluable, but sometimes changes and variations do exist as catalogs are often made up before the dolls are produced. They are a valuable research tool, but are not infallible. Also, clip the advertisements for the store specials you buy.They will be of great interest to you in the future. The more you know about Alexander dolls, the more you will enjoy collecting them.

9.Restoration has made many excellent dolls near mint. Study publications that show you how to revamp hair, textiles and fabrics. NEVER however, practice on an expensive older doll. There are many opinions on how much, if anything, to do to "fix-up an older doll. Listen to the options and opinions and then decide what your personal philosophy will be. It is YOUR collection and it should reflect YOUR ideals and standards.

10. Finally, don't overlook the fellowship

A 14in (36cm) all composition *Margaret O'Brien* is a collector's dream. In addition to being in "mint as new" condition, she has her clover leaf wrist tag with her name. *A. Glenn Mandeville Collection.*

and friendships that doll collecting offers. The doll show circuit is filled with people just like yourself. There are conventions devoted to Madame Alexander dolls, and ads placed by other collectors. One thing I have learned is that doll collectors seem to gravitate to each other. Lifestyles, age and wealth, are not the barrier to doll relationships as they are in the outside world. DO reach out to just one collector and I'll bet within a month, you will find more new friends than you could ever imagine!

Yes the world of doll collecting is a wonderful, fun filled place. With a little effort, time and education, you can learn the history behind the beautiful dolls. Why not make your collection reflect the very best that life has to offer? Doll collecting, especially Madame Alexander doll, makes life a great deal of fun! Start your collection today!

Alexander Doll Faces

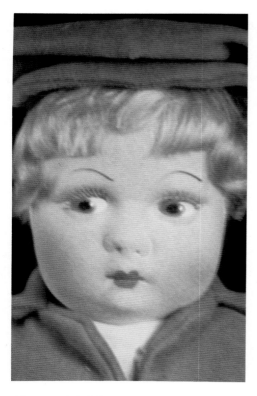

The pressed cloth face shown here was the first doll face used by the Alexander Doll Company in the 1920s and into the early 1930s. Unmarked, it has a swivel neck. Most were hand painted by Madame and her sisters! *A. Glenn Mandeville Collection.*

The Alexander Doll Company has produced thousand of dolls over a span of seventy years! Known as a fashion designer and not a doll artist, Madame Alexander created most of her often award winning characters out of a few basic doll faces. Some characters, especially celebrities like *Jane Withers, Sonja Henie*, and *Shari Lewis*, had a unique head designed for the company. Most of the never-ending parade of art and literary figures, storybook and nursery rhyme characters, and beloved dolls of royalty and film stars, were brought to life with the skilled use of a combination of clothing design, hairstyles and make-up. It is a cherished tradition that continues today.

Here in our photo gallery are some famous faces that have been used for three quarters of a century. Look carefully at the faces, for while featured here, the next time you see it, that face may belong to a Prince, a Queen, a fairy tale character or even your favorite movie star!

It is not often important to identify an undressed Alexander doll. Frankly, as Madame would often say, "My figures (dolls) are merely the mannequins upon which I drape my dreams."

Clothing labels, wrist tags, (which are often dated) and research will tell more of a doll's history than a face alone.

Some generalizations with exceptions apply. Cloth dolls were unmarked, but jointed at the neck and used from the 1920s into the 1930s. Composition dolls (a mixture of sawdust, and glue, and then painted) were the mainstay of doll making until the late 1940s. Hard plastic, especially on a larger doll, generally dates the doll from the 1950s. Soft vinyl plastic on a larger doll usually means the doll is more contemporary. One notable exception is the 8in (20cm) all hard plastic doll, Introduced as *Wendy Ann* in 1953. It still is being made today.

As with many doll companies, the date incised on the doll is the year the mold was made and not the particular date of the character that utilized that mold. As many as three decades can pass and a date will remain the same if that mold is still being used. As stated before, costuming and hairstyling are essential to identifying an Alexander doll.

The author would recommend the following grading system when buying, selling, or insuring your dolls.

MINT...a VERY overused term. In actuality, about 15% of older dolls advertised or shown for sale fit the definition of this

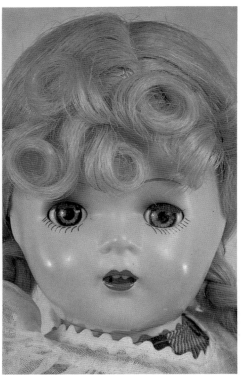

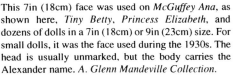

This 7in (18cm) face was used on *McGuffey Ana*, as shown here, *Tiny Betty*, *Princess Elizabeth*, and dozens of dolls in a 7in (18cm) or 9in (23cm) size. For small dolls, it was the face used during the 1930s. The head is usually unmarked, but the body carries the Alexander name. *A. Glenn Mandeville Collection.*

A stunning *McGuffey Ana* shows yet another face used in the late 1930s and is usually marked with the "Princess Elizabeth" and Alexander name. This head mold was primarily used in the late 1930s and early 1940s on larger size dolls. *A. Glenn Mandeville Collection.*

word. A mint doll should look like it did when it left the factory, whether 70 minutes or 70 years ago! That "crisp" feeling to the clothing should be there. Facial coloring would be bright and fresh. The wig or rooted hairstyle must be undisturbed. This type of doll is not seen as often as one would expect with the overuse of this term. Naturally, an original box (a blessing to some collectors, and a burden to others) would add more value, as would a catalog, wrist tag, hat box, or any other accessory sold with the doll.

EXCELLENT...About 20% of dolls seen today, barring new releases are in this condition. To some, MINT and EXCELLENT are the same. To the advanced collector they are not. These

terms also do NOT apply to a doll with "replaced" anything. Avoid using the phrase, "excellent, but". They can't coexist! Your excellent dolls would have everything all original but perhaps lack that extra sparkle and crispness of a never handled doll.

GOOD...There is certainly nothing wrong with a doll in good condition. In my opinion, the bulk of dolls found today should be graded using this word. The term, "good," as it applies to food, is certainly not a negative and with an Alexander doll it should not be either. A constant source of conflict between buyer and seller is that the term "mint" has been used to describe a doll in really "good" condition. The collector of "mint" dolls generally is not looking for

Known for captivating collectors, this delicate face came wigged with painted hair. It was used for 12in (31cm) versions of *Wendy-Ann*, *Alice in Wonderland* and a few other rare characters. The body has a swivel waist and posed hands. The Alexander name is most often found on the doll. *A. Glenn Mandeville Collection.*

Sonja Henie was the wealthiest woman in the world in the 1930s. In order to secure the rights to manufacture a *Sonja Henie* doll, Madame had to present a special mold. This mold was used for the *Sonja Henie* dolls, some World War II military dolls and a bride doll. It bears the name of the skating star. *A. Glenn Mandeville Collection.*

"good" condition dolls, even for a fair price. They would prefer a "mint" doll and should be willing to pay for it. Likewise, many collectors of "good" condition dolls do not want the expense or responsibility of a "mint" doll which must be carefully handled in order to keep its grading at "mint".

A "good" condition doll would have original clothing, shoes and maybe just need some surface cleaning. To be in good condition, an Alexander doll should not have badly laundered or replaced clothing, cut hair or missing important accessories. In reality, "good" dolls are quite desirable to many collectors.

Those who sell dolls would fair far better if price and condition matched each other. Once again, educating people that an intelligent grading system can work is the key.

FAIR...While many Alexander dolls are bought to be "shelf dolls" or just brought out on special occasions, many, many dolls were loved and cherished by countless children. Many collectors LOVE "fair' condition dolls, AND the low prices that they SHOULD have. At the very least, one half of the listed value is subtracted for a doll in "fair" condition. Once a stigma in collecting, skilled collectors often are quite thrilled to find a pre-loved doll and restore it to as close to mint condition as possible. The skill level of this group of collectors is astonishing!

Margaret O'Brien was the child star of the new decade, the 1940s. Her likeness, usually marked ALEX on the head, was used in both composition and hard plastic from the 1940s into the early 1950s. It was a face that launched a thousand ships! *A. Glenn Mandeville Collection.*

Virtually the same face, only in a larger size and in the new hard plastic, this face mold first used on the *Margaret O'Brien* dolls would become the standard of beauty for the Alexander Doll Company. *A. Glenn Mandeville Collection.*

Dolls that once would be overlooked are getting a new lease on life and making a new owner proud! This classification, in my opinion, is the one that causes the most pricing problems. A used child's toy is NOT a coveted, mint condition art object and should be priced as such. Unless very rare, it would be hard to justify a price over $300 for a doll in pre-loved condition. As stated, don't overpay, whether for yourself or for resale, for many collectors would rather settle for no example of a doll than take a less than mint doll at any price. Once you have mastered this concept, you are on your way to a successful hobby or business. I have found that doll collectors are a special breed of people. Most are more than willing to share their knowledge!

POOR...This is an often overlooked category, that affords the collector a great opportunity. Actually some dolls that are labeled in poor condition might have a fantastic wig, or original shoes. This type of doll is usually bought for "parts" for a "good" or "fair" condition doll. If you are interested in "good," or "fair" condition dolls, don't overlook a doll graded as "poor." It just might have the missing accessory you have been searching for!

As you can see, grading an Alexander doll is really quite simple as long as you remain knowledgeable about a few facts!

1. You can never make a doll "mint." It can be skillfully restored to excellent

Often unmarked, this full cheeked unmistakable face was used in hard plastic in the early 1950s for Kate Smith's *Annabelle, Maggie Teenager, Peter Pan, Little Women, Little Men,* and many others such as brides and bridesmaids. Most of the larger size dolls used either this face or the mold first used on *Margaret O'Brien. A. Glenn Mandeville Collection.*

Cissy was Madame Alexander's entry into the world of high fashion. This face, which usually bears the Alexander Company markings, was used on child dolls such as *Binnie* and *Winnie Walker* and some of the early 1960s Portrait dolls. *Cissy* was a powerful presence in the Alexander line-up. *A. Glenn Mandeville Collection.*

condition but the very term "mint" implies seamless perfection. Do not decide to collect only "mint" dolls unless you are willing to pay top prices for the very best examples. The term "mint-reasonable" has no place in a doll wanted ad!

2. Learn all you can about the "tricks of the trade." Techniques such as using boiling water to restore hair sets and laundry methods that are state of the art, can give you a VERY fine collection at an attractive price!

3. Do realize that "good" condition dolls are NOT the step-children of collecting. Just as some collectors want only mint dolls, others are turned off by dolls they feel they can never undress, handle or display. There is no right or wrong in a hobby, it is your choice.

4. Do try to convince anyone who will listen that pricing an Alexander doll is just like pricing a comic book or other collectible. The condition is everything. Certainly never pay a near-mint price for a played with doll.

5. While all price guides say that a guide is just that, do remember that many, many variables influence the price of a doll. Prices vary greatly throughout the country. A major doll convention in a particular area can also affect pricing. Special dolls vary greatly in price as the

Often described as coy and cute, this vinyl face was used on several girl dolls of the late 1950s, such as *Marybell, The Doll Who Gets Well, Country Cousins, Kelly* and *Pollyanna*. She bears the Alexander marking on her head. *A. Glenn Mandeville Collection.*

An impish grin in hard plastic, 8in (20cm) style, is *Maggie Mix-up* made in 1960-1961. While unmarked, this head is once again a collector favorite in the 1990s. Her smile was used on angels, devils and other assorted characters of fame and fable! The body has the Alexander Doll Company name. *A. Glenn Mandeville Collection.*

good time associated with the event sometimes gets added to the price. Remember that it is your money, your hobby and your life! Learn all you can about everything. Network with other collectors and I'll bet you will wind up with an outstanding collection, no matter what your taste and level of collecting may be.

Today is an exciting time for the collector of Madame Alexander dolls. There are all types of dolls, new and old, for just about any taste or budget. There are mint as new dolls, as well as some real "handyman's specials." Doll shows and events that feature Madame Alexander dolls occur just about every weekend! It's a doll's life out there! Why not get started today? With the popularity of Madame Alexander dolls, should your path change and you wake up one day and thinking WHY are all my dolls blonde or brides or whatever, you can sell your dolls to eager collectors and go off in another direction. Doll collecting is one of the few areas of your life today where you are in total control! That's what makes it so much fun to "children" of all ages! In my experience, the friendships made while collecting dolls are long lasting and solid. There is a whole world of interesting people, places and dolls to see!

Note: In future editions, different faces will be highlighted in order to complete your Alexander gallery of famous stars! To most collectors, the costume is the character, a proud tradition which continues today.

Another famous face is this mold that was originally used in 1957 on *Cissette*, a 10in (25cm) full figured doll, and then with heavy make-up for this *Jacqueline*. Friends *Margot, Gold Rush, Klondike Kate* and other worldly women were created from these enchanting molds. Still a popular favorite, this perky lady is the face used on the *Portrette Series*, both in the 1960s as well as the current line. The body bears the Alexander Company markings. *A. Glenn Mandeville Collection.*

Often called "The Face," this 8in (20cm) darling is the masthead of the Alexander Star Fleet! Originally used in 1953, this face, in one form or another, is still the *Wendy That Loves Being Loved!* The head is unmarked but the body bears the Alexander Company name. *A. Glenn Mandeville Collection.*

Always a classic in hard plastic, this *McGuffey Ana* uses the face that collectors now call *Classic Lissy*, meaning that the name *Lissy* was the most often nomenclature attached to this pursed lip pretty! Her face today makes *Hans* and *Gretl Brinker* quite a pair. In the 1960s, she was everything from *Scarlett O'Hara* in a 12in (31cm) size, to demure little girls. This head is unmarked but with a marked Alexander body. *A. Glenn Mandeville Collection.*

Introduced as a versatile 12in (31cm) vinyl young lady in the late 1960s, this face was utilized on the hard plastic body still in use today.From *Nancy Drew*, teen detective, to *Little Women*, this is indeed a famous visage! What other face could be **BOTH** *Scarlett* and *Rhett*, *Napoleon* and *Josephine*, *Antony* and *Cleopatra*, AND *Lord Fauntleroy!* Marked with the Alexander Company markings on the neck, this face was another classic like the face used on the 8in (20cm) dolls. These faces were very versatile and chameleon like in character creation. *A. Glenn Mandeville Collection.*

One of a long line of famous faces, this vinyl little girl first appeared in the mid 1960s and is still being used today. Always a 14in (36cm) size, she carries the Alexander Company markings on her neck. From *First Lady* to *McGuffey Ana*, *Alice* to *Little Orphant Annie*, this face is another Alexander doll star! *A. Glenn Mandeville Collection.*

The 21in (53cm) *Portrait* dolls started in the 1960s, are the frosting on the cake for most collectors who would want more were it not for their imposing size. Marked on the back of the neck with the Alexander Company name, this doll was once *Jacqueline* of Camelot days, *Marie Antoinette* and enough classic characters to fill the finest of art galleries! *A. Glenn Mandeville Collection.*

17

Alexander Doll Designers

Daun Fallon

"My memory of my own 8in (20cm) *Ballerina* was probably responsible for my career choice as a Costume Designer." Daun fondly recalls. Working as a Broadway costume designer, Daun brings a vast quantity and quality of talent and imagination to the Alexander Doll Designers team. Add to that a vivid memory of a *Wendy* doll in pink sequins and it isn't hard to see where the award-nominated dolls such as *Tinkerbell*, *The Goldfish*, *The Scarlet Series* and all of our friends from Oz have merged.

Therese J. Stadelmeier

Therese Stadelmeier always had a passion for dolls and costume designing. She owned her first Alexander at the age of four and started her early designing career by creating an Abigail Adams costume for her Barbie® soon after that. She too created many costumes for Broadway shows before joining the designing team in 1991. Describing her work as "getting to live out every little girl's fantasy," Therese has been the proud designer of such Alexander successes as the *Anne* and *Wendy Loves...* series among many others, several of which have received *Doll Reader®* magazine's DOTY® and *Dolls* magazine Award of Excellence nominations.

Preserving Your Alexander Dolls

Collectors of Alexander dolls have often been referred to as "perfectionists." In many cases this is true. The collector who has chosen to pay the price for mint-in-box dolls, must, by definition, be somewhat of a perfectionist. AND, it would be necessary for that collector to keep being that way to maintain the "mint" grading of their dolls.

All this might sound pretty intimidating to the novice collector, or the casual reader of this book, but it IS possible to maintain any Alexander doll collection at the purchase level with just some good advice and plain common sense.

My own Alexander collection is made up of a few perfect mint-in-box dolls, that I must admit, intimidate me a bit. We have been taught that the word "investment" implies perfection but that is only true some of the time.

A couple of years ago, The Alexander Doll Company began a series of 8in (20cm) dolls dressed as angels. Casually titled "Tree Toppers" they were perfection itself. Speigel's has had exclusives and The Alexander Doll Company has issued some of its own.

When I got my first doll from Spiegel's, the sheer wonder of that perfect little angelic tree topper in the box was awesome! It took me a week to get up the nerve to just remove the neck brace, which was stapled to the sides of the box. (If you don't understand any of this, then you are truly a new collector or a casual observer.)

Finally, when I removed that incredible creature and put her where she belonged, on top of my Christmas tree, I felt like a recovering "never take it from the box" collector! The happiness that doll brought to me, my family, my neighbors and friends, would fill this book. My friends noticed my OTHER dolls and even my family was spellbound by the majesty that this Tree Topper dealt from her lofty place!

After the holidays, I carefully returned my little angel to her box and lo and behold, guess what! She had not suffered a bit! Her gown was still radiant; her halo angelic; and her pursed lips were still serene! I had broken the spell of the boxed doll! She had survived and so had I!

The moral of this story is that even the highest quality mint-in-box Alexander doll CAN be enjoyed out of its box AND not suffer in the hands of a skilled collector. One has to remember that one does own their doll collection and not the other way around!

One of the nicer things about Alexander dolls, for the most part, is that they are not shrink wrapped and sealed in boxes. Unlike some other dolls (notably fashion dolls) they can be removed from their boxes, observed, photographed, gently handled and still not lose their "mint" grading. They are not held prisoner by cellophane and cardboard, but float loose in the box, to be set free by the new owner.

In one of my early encounters with Madame Alexander at a doll show in New England in the late 1970s, I asked Madame why her doll boxes did not portray the gorgeous artwork that fashion dolls, character dolls, and celebrity dolls did? Smiling, Madame said that the box was, and I quote, "merely the shipping carton for the doll to arrive safely from us to you. We are creating dolls, NOT boxes!" Well, I guess I knew from then on that an Alexander box is not the shrine that some collectors make it out to be!

How then can the collector who is buying a "mint" graded doll enjoy it without destroying it? Easy! There are just a few, simple rules!

Finally, don't you think that it's time we started ENJOYING our dolls more? I

Rarely does one find a composition Alexander doll in such incredible condition. This 1930s vintage *McGuffey Ana* is all original, complete with her "schoolhouse" wrist tag. She did not come with a hat as shown on her wrist tag. Keeping her in excellent condition involves common sense as outlined in this chapter! *A. Glenn Mandeville Collection.*

give programs all over the United States and I love photographing my own dolls, the dolls that come through my business and my friends' dolls. Never once in twenty years, has a doll suffered during a photo shoot. If anything, I examined the doll more closely before the photo and tamed a stray hair, or fluffed up a dress. Like us, dolls seem to thrive on love and attention.

I guess the above mentioned topics will ruffle some feathers from the "don't touch" crowd, but as I stated, none of my dolls have ever suffered from careful display and handling, while I have had

clothing disintegrate from acids in the box! The bottom line is, enjoy your dolls, and I think your doll collecting will be a whole lot more fun! I sure think so and I'll bet you will too!

ABBREVIATIONS

MADC = Madame Alexander Doll Club
LE = Limited Edition
FAD = Factory Altered Doll
EDH = Enchanted Doll House
CU = Collector's United
UFDC = United Federation of Doll Clubs
NECS = New England Collector's Society
S/A = Still Available
N/A = Information not available

Simple Rules to Preserve Alexander Dolls

1 If you do buy a mint in box Alexander doll, whether old or new, replace the tissue paper with acid-free tissue. This can be found at art supply houses, craft stores and even dry cleaners that specialize in wedding gown cleaning. This will prevent the acid in the tissue and cardboard from reacting with the fabric and the doll. Surprised? Yes, the box is NOT often the best place for your doll to be kept! If the original tissue captivates you, put it in a baggie and keep it in the box, which can be collapsed and stored.

2 Sunlight, even normal room light, is a real enemy of dolls. Fabrics fade gradually. Sometimes it isn't until you take a doll out of a cabinet years later that you notice the sun has faded the front of the doll's outfit. This does NOT mean that you can never have a doll on display in a "normal" room. Just be sure direct sunlight does not hit the doll and rotate the dolls in the room from time to time. Seasonal displays are one reason to collect dolls. Don't deny yourself the pleasure of a holiday display out of fear of harming your doll. Common sense is the password.

3 Children, pets and dolls do not mix. They can, but keep the dolls high and the rest low! Seriously, your five year old can't tell that your *Cissy* is over thirty years old. You can also be sure that the plastic still smells mighty good to your "man's best friend," so prevention is the key. Don't mix the deadly triangle of pets, plastic and pretty children!

4 As mentioned above, enjoy your dolls. Why have them, if they are just listed in a notebook and stuffed in a closet? (Sometimes they don't even make a notebook!) Great that you went to Disney World® and stayed up all night to get that Alexander exclusive! Now what? Put the precious thing under a dome, or in a display and love it to death! That IS why you bought it, isn't it?

5 Despite what some well meaning curators and gloom and doom "experts" say, sensible handling and displaying of your dolls will NOT make them lose a grade. For the collector of "good" condition dolls, this may be a chapter they think they can skip over. NOT SO! Any doll, if exposed to sunlight, insects, pets, extremes in temperature and ill handling (from the very young on up), CAN suffer greatly. I often think of a doll as a wonderful piece of jewelry. It enhances the owner's beauty, when worn and displayed, but does nothing in a safety deposit box except tarnish! It's the same with dolls!

Little Women...
A timeless tale of dolls and devotion

I vividly remember the first time I read Louisa May Alcott's story of *Little Women*. I was in eighth grade, and was looking forward to reading it, about as much as a toddler wants a plate of spinach.

Yet alone in my room, I remember being spellbound by the intricacy of the story, that to me, was one of survival, growth, pride and togetherness in the face of hardships. The characters were wonderful; spun of brilliant mind and woven of strong, yet very real fibers. My book report was graded "A" because my instant love with this tale translated into my work. I would not be the only youth to feel that way about this book, *Little Women*.

When I had the privilege to meet Madame Alexander for the first time in Connecticut in the 1970s, I asked her what her favorite stories were. It took her little time to answer that *Gone with the Wind* and *Little Women* were among her favorites. Both had elements of strong female characters obligated to function in a male dominated world, with not much social or legal status. Forced to be independent, the many heroines of both these books represented not only women, but human beings at their finest. Scarlett may have had her selfish moments but she was a survivor.

The Lissy molds were used on a set of *Little Women* dolls that were 12in (31cm) tall and all hard plastic issued in 1993. This is *Jo*. Note the beautiful blush and the highly detailed outfit. This set of *Little Women* dolls was a personal favorite. *A. Glenn Mandeville collection.*

Neither Scarlett nor Jo let a lack of money or convenient circumstances prevent them from doing what they had to do. To me, and obviously to Madame Alexander, *Little Women* was a saga of survival and struggle, without losing one's principles and values.

Actually it was that meeting with Madame Alexander that changed the course of my life. It gave me the push I needed to start my own business and pursue the dreams I had carried since childhood. I wanted society to see dolls as an art form worthy of the finest collections, preserved by both men and women, and not merely a toy to be discarded later in life. I wanted to help preserve the rich cultural heritage that I feel is often told in a collection of children's playthings, designed and marketed by adults.

Madame Alexander loved to read, and usually after she had read something interesting, she would try to translate that into a clothing design for her "mannequins", as she often referred to her dolls. The legacy she left to us, was the staggering ability to create thousands of characters based on a few basic dolls that she did not design, but turned into the personification of her active imagination. Madame Alexander was a true fashion designer in the purist sense.

The first Little Women dolls appeared in the early 1930s in cloth form with hand painted features done by

Madame and her sisters. They are very difficult to find today in mint condition today. In my early business days, I had a set of the four dolls, mint-in-box with wrist tags. Being young and not as appreciative of art as I am today, I let them go and have never seen a set to equal them since. The clothing was as complicated as Walter Plunkett design, yet had the homespun simplicity that made the Little Women dolls a success.

The dolls appeared again in the late 1930s in a smaller composition size, packed in a flowered gift box. They were an instant hit to a Depression and war weary nation who wanted to believe in the ideals of the past.

Madame had seen and loved the 1933 MGM version on film of *Little Women,* starring Katherine Hepburn and featuring my personal favorite, Joan Bennett. (She would later play a BIG part in my life in the 1960s soap opera, "Dark Shadows").

The cloth dolls and the small composition dolls were issued in conjunction with this movie. The Alexander Doll Company was one of the industry leaders to use the new hard plastic material for doll making, and in the late 1940s issued probably the most coveted set of Little Women dolls, using just two molds in a 14in (36cm) size with delicate and fragile embroidery floss wigs. Some stores had special costumes and many variations exist. The dolls were made with the small, closed hands for several years and soon Marme, the loyal

The Columbia Pictures 1994 version of *Little Women* gave collectors a first! A set of all five characters in 8in (20cm) hard plastic were issued in authentic movie costume with the movie poster as a wrist tag. They were an exclusive to FAO Schwarz. *A. Glenn Mandeville collection.*

and caring mother to the March family, would be added to the set.

Little Women fans were delighted when MGM again decided to retell the Louisa May Alcott fable in 1949. This version featured costumes by Walter Plunkett of Gone with the Wind fame and was "old Hollywood" at its glamourous best. Poverty and misfortune never looked better than it did on June Allyson, Janet Leigh, Elizabeth Taylor and a tear jerking Margaret O'Brien, as Beth. The movie, like the story itself, was filmed with tremendous care. The painted glass backdrops and the long distance camera angles, focused on the struggle of a family determined to move forward in the midst of chaos.

The Little Women dolls captured all the beauty of the costumes detailed in the book. During the 1950s they were made in the same size, but with open, larger hands, and new Saran wigs. As usual, Madame's designs were based on her interpretations of the book and her imagination of what the character would be wearing. Madame reveled in intense period fashion research. The release of the dolls to coincide with the movie was a business strategy. It was one that the Company would use many times. Madame Alexander always realized that a craftsman without an audience performs only to himself. Unlike many artists, she was conscious of the necessary balance between creativity and profit. It was seldom that catalogs did not feature a set of

Madame Alexander Little Women dolls, as each new generation of children read the adventures of a Civil War family and their rich tapestry of life.

By the 1960s, the Alexander Doll Company had won the race to capture the miniature doll market with its 8in (20cm) *Wendy* doll. Never has a clothing designer done more with a mannequin than Madame Alexander did with this demure, sweet faced little doll that began in 1953.

Throughout the 1960s, the Little Women dolls would be available in not only the 8in (20cm) size, but in exquisite 12in (31cm) versions first with a hard plastic head, and then with the standard vinyl head used on the dolls for well over twenty years.

In the turbulent 1970s and the so-called excessive 1980s, Alexander Company catalogs showed a continual flow of Little Women dolls, with various costuming and size changes. They were a constant in a world of change.

Collectors today often have difficulty in finding a matched set of dolls from one year because many children received one doll for a birthday and then perhaps another for a religious holiday or some other family tradition. It often might have taken a child several years to complete the set, which is why so many private collections have dolls in different year costumes. It is a collecting paradox that such a set holds so much sentimental value and historical perspective, yet the monetary worth is not the same as if the set were from the same issue. Fortunately, many Little Women sets stayed the same over very long periods of time, especially the 8in (20cm) and the 12in (31cm) dolls so it is possible to find some of these complete groupings as shown in the company catalogs.

In 1994 state of the art technology once again brought the movie *Little Women* to the forefront in the Columbia Pictures version featuring Winona Rider who was nominated for an Academy Award for Best Actress in her role as Jo. The commercial success of this period movie once again proves that the values explored are still valid. The film's advanced technology made the viewers feel that they really had gone back in time to a dreadful part of American history.

For this occasion, The Alexander Doll Company created a boxed set of five 8in (20cm) dolls in authentic movie costumes with wrist tags featuring the movie poster. Packed in one box and made under license, this set is a real rarity in the company's history. It is the first known set of Little Women dolls to feature authentic costumes from one of the film versions. These 500 sets made exclusively for FAO Schwarz will be a valued collectible in the future.

The Alexander Doll Company also has a gorgeous set of 8in (20cm) Little Women dolls that are part of the regular 1995 line and available through your retailer.

It is refreshing and comforting to know that the saga of the March family's Little Women is not only as popular as ever, but also that survival and independent growth can occur in the midst of chaos. All one needs is a strong foundation. Parents today would be wise to instill these values in their children for they are everlasting no matter what century it may be. Adults too, can benefit from the messages of quiet strength told on the pages of this delightful tale.

The Alexander Doll Company has continued to take the rich traditions of the past and blend them with today. It is nice to know that in a hectic, fast paced world, the past and the present can mesh in a collection of Little Women dolls by The Alexander Doll Company. If the older dolls are out of your price range then by all means take advantage of the current offerings, as these dolls, like those who came before them, will be the collectibles of tomorrow. Your video store has the 1933 and the 1949 movie versions on film. The 1994 version is due to be released soon. Once you see the story, you will never forget it. Your Little Women dolls will then hold a special place in your doll display. Why not start your collection today?

Twenty One Special Years of Special Dolls

(See page 28 for separate listing of 1994 Special Dolls)

Compiled by Benita Schwartz

YEAR	NAME OF DOLL & SIZE	PRODUCED FOR	OTHER INFORMATION
1992	My Little Sweetheart 8" (20cm)	**A Child at Heart**	LE of 4,000, 4 Hair Colors
1992	My Little Sweetheart 8" (20cm)	A Child at Heart	LE of 500, Black Skin
1993	Trick and Treat 8" (20cm) pair	A Child at Heart	
1993	Now I Know My ABC's 8" (20cm)	**ABC Unlimited Productions**	
1988	Miss Scarlett 14" (36cm)	**Belk & Leggett**	N/A
1989	Rachel 8" (20cm)	Belk & Leggett	N/A
1992	Annabelle 8" (20cm)	Belk & Leggett	LE of 3,000
1993	Caroline 8" (20cm)	Belk & Leggett	
1991	David, the Little Rabbi 8" (20cm)	**Celia's Dolls**	LE of 3,600 3 Hair Colors
1992	Alpine Christmas Twins 8" (20cm)	**Christmas Shoppe**	LE of 2,000, 5 Hair Color Combinations
1992	Le Petit Boudoir 10" (25cm)	**Collector's United**	LE of 700
1991	Camelot in Columbia 8" (20cm)	**Columbia Show**	FAD of 400
1987	Yugoslavia 8" (20cm)	**CU Gathering**	FAD
1988	Tippi 8" (20cm)	CU Gathering	LE of 800
1989	Miss Leigh 8" (20cm)	CU Gathering	LE of 800
1992	Faith 8" (20cm)	CU Gathering	LE of 800
1993	Hope 8" (20cm)	CU Gathering	
1972-1976	Alice 8" (20cm)	**Disney®**	Bend Knee or Straight Leg
1972-1976	Snow White 8" (20cm)	Disney®	Bent Knee or Straight Leg
1973	Tinkerbell 8" (20cm)	Disney®	Straight Leg
1989	Cinderella 10" (25cm)	Disney®	LE of 250
1989	Sleeping Beauty 21" (53cm)	Disney World® Auction	One-of-a-Kind
1991	Alice and the White Rabbit 10" (25cm)	Disney World®	LE of 750
1991	Mouseketeer 8" (20cm)	Disney®	N/A
1991	Queen Isabella 21" (53cm)	Disney World® Auction	One-of-a-Kind
1992	Emperor & Nightingale**	Disney World® Auction, Teddy Bear & Doll Convention	One-of-a-Kind
1992	It's A Girl 21" (53cm)	Disney World® Auction, Teddy Bear & Doll Convention	One-of-a-Kind
1992	Queen of Hearts 10" (25cm)	Disney World®	LE of 500
1992	Queen of Hearts 10" (25cm) Plays Croquette	Disney World®	
1992	Round Up Day Mouseketeer 8" (20cm)	Disney®	N/A
1992	Thoroughly Modern Wendy 8" (20cm)	Disney®	
1993	Alice & the Jabberwocky 12" (31cm) cloth animals	Disney World®, Teddy Bear & Doll Convention	
1993	Annette 14" (36cm) porcelain doll	Disney® License	
1993	Frog and Frog Princess 18" (46cm) Steiff Bear & an 8" (20cm) Alexander Doll	Disney World® Auction Teddy Bear & Doll Convention	One-of-a-Kind
1993	Snow White 10" (25cm)	Disney® License	
1993	Women in the Garden 10" (25cm) four dolls	Disney World®, Teddy Bear & Doll Convention	One-of-a-Kind
1993	Cissy Bride 1921 21" (53cm) companions 8" (20cm) two	**Disneyland Auction**	One-of-a-Kind
1993	Monique 8" (20cm)	Disneyland Teddy Bear & Doll Classic	
1991	Pandora 8" (20cm)	**Dolls in Bearland**	LE of Approx. 1,800

YEAR	NAME OF DOLL & SIZE	PRODUCED FOR	OTHER INFORMATION
1992	Susannah 8" (20cm)	**Dolly Dears**	LE of 400
1993	Jack Be Nimble 8" (20cm)	Dolly Dears	
1993	Princess & the Pea 8" (20cm)	Dolly Dears	Mattress sold separately
1980	The Enchanted Doll 8" (20cm)	**EDH**	LE of 3,000, Lace Trim
1981	The Enchanted Doll 8" (20cm)	EDH	LE of 3,423, Eyelet Trim
1983	Ballerina Trunk Set 8" (20cm)	EDH	Blue or Pink Tutu
1985	Cinderella & Trunk 14" (36cm)	EDH	Comes w/Glass Slipper
1988	The Enchanted Doll 10" (25cm)	EDH	LE of 5,000
1989	Ballerina 8" (20cm)	EDH	LE of 360, Blue Tutu
1991	Farmer's Daughter 8" (20cm)	EDH	LE of 4,000 3 Hair Colors
1992	Farmer's Daughter Goes to Town 8" (20cm)	EDH	LE of 1,600 3 Hair Colors
1987	Pussycat 18" (46cm)	**FAO Schwarz**	Pale Blue Dress & Bonnet
1988	Brooke 14" (36cm)	FAO Schwarz	Blonde or Brunette Hair
1989	David & Diana 8" (20cm)	FAO Schwarz	Comes with Wagon
1989	Samantha 14" (36cm)	FAO Schwarz	N/A
1991	Beddy-Bye Brooke 14" (36cm)	FAO Schwarz	N/A
1991	Carnevale 14" (36cm)	FAO Schwarz	N/A
1992	Beddy-Bye Brooke & Brenda	FAO Schwarz	Matching 14" (36cm) & 8" (20cm) Pair
1993	Wendy Shops at FAO Schwarz 8" (20cm)	FAO Schwarz	
1992	Oktoberfest 8" (20cm)	**Greenville Show**	FAD of 200
1992	Oktoberfest Boy 8" (20cm)	Greenville Show	FAD of 6
1991	Melody & Friend 8" (20cm) and 26" (66cm)	**Günzel**	LE of 1,000*
1992	Courtney & Friends	Günzel	LE of 1,200*
1993	Harmony & Cherub 21" (53cm) and 8" (20cm)	Günzel	
1993	Pamela Plays Dress-Up at Grandma's 12" (31cm)	**Horchow**	
1991	Miss Magnin 10" (25cm)	**I. Magnin**	LE of 2,500
1992	Little Huggum 12" (31cm)	I. Magnin	LE of 1,500, Has Cradle
1992	Little Miss Magnin 8" (20cm)	I. Magnin	LE of 3,600, 2 Hair Colors
1993	Bon Voyage Little Miss Magnin 8" (20cm)	I. Magnin	
1993	Bon Voyage Miss Magnin 10" (25cm)	I. Magnin	
1991	Little Huggums 12" (31cm)	**Imaginarium**	2 Hair Colors, Also Bald
1992	Suellen 12" (31cm)	**Jean's Dolls**	FAD of 192, Blonde Hair
1984	Ballerina 8" (20cm)	**MADC Convention**	FAD of 360
1985	Happy Birthday Madame 8" (20cm)	MADC Convention	FAD of 450
1986	Scarlett 8" (20cm)	MADC Convention	FAD of 625, Red Ribbon Trim
1987	Cowboy 8" (20cm)	MADC Convention	LE of 720
1988	Flapper 10" (25cm)	MADC Convention	FAD of 720, Black
1992	Drucilla 14" (36cm)	MADC Convention	FAD of Approx. 250
1992	Prom Queen 8" (20cm)	MADC Convention	LE of 1,100
1993	Anastasia 14" (36cm)	MADC Convention	FAD
1993	Diamond Lil 10" (25cm)	MADC Convention	
1991	Miss Liberty 10" (25cm)	**MADC Club Doll**	N/A
1992	Little Miss Godey 8" (20cm)	MADC Club Doll	N/A
1993	Wendy Loves Being Best Friends 8" (20cm)	MADC Club Doll	
1992	Wintertime 8" (20cm)	**MADC Premiere**	LE of 1,650
1993	Homecoming 8" (20cm)	MADC Premiere	
1992	Spring Break 8" (20cm)	**Metroplex Show**	LE of 400
1992	Queen Elizabeth II 8" (20cm)	**Mid-Year Release**	N/A
1992	Wendy Loves Being Loved 8" (20cm)	Mid-Year Release	3 Hair Colors

YEAR	NAME OF DOLL & SIZE	PRODUCED FOR	OTHER INFORMATION
1991	Welcome Home 8" (20cm)	Mid-Year Release	2 Hair Colors, Boy or Girl, Black or White
1989	Southern Belle 10" (25cm)	**My Doll House**	Blonde or Brunette
1991	Empress Elisabeth 10" (25cm)	My Doll House	N/A
1992	Winter Wonderland II 8" (20cm)	**Nashville Show**	FAD of 200, Skier
1993	Carline's Storyland Trunk 8" (20cm)	**Neiman Marcus**	
1993	Saks Own Christmas Carol 8" (20cm)	**Saks Fifth Avenue**	
1991	Winter Sports 8" (20cm)	**Shirley's Dollhouse**	FAD of 975
1993	Wendy Visits the World's Fair 8" (20cm)	Shirley's Dollhouse	
1993	Winter Angel 8" (20cm)	Shirley's Dollhouse	FAD
1993	Texas Shriner 8" (20cm)	**Shriner's National Convention,** San Antonio, Texas	
1991	Merry Angel 8" (20cm)	**Spiegel**	Christmas Tree Topper
1992	Joy Noel Tree Topper 10" (25cm)	Spiegel	LE of 3,000
1992	Mardi Gras 10" (25cm)	Spiegel	LE of 3,000
1991	Miss Unity 10" (25cm)	**UFDC Luncheon**	LE of 310
1992	Little Emperor 8" (20cm)	UFDC Luncheon	LE of 400
1993	Columbian Sailor 12" (31cm)	UFDC Luncheon	
1992	Bathing Beauty 10" (25cm)	**UFDC Regional**	LE of 300

*Doll Artist Hildegard Günzel has created limited edition porcelain dolls. Some come with Madame Alexander Dolls. *Melody's Friend* is an 8" (20cm) Wendy dressed to match. Courtney comes with two 8" (20cm) Alexander-kins, a boy and a girl, dressed in coordinating outfits.

**The Emperor and The Nightingale* is a joint effort by Gund and the Alexander Doll Company. *The Emperor* is a Gund teddy bear dressed in an oriental costume created by the Alexander Doll Company designers. The *Nightingale* is an 8" (20cm) Wendy doll.

The Lissy mold, made famous in the 1950s and 1960s, was used for this great all hard plastic 12in (31cm) *Alice and the Jabberwocky*, available for purchase to registered guests at the 1993 Walt Diney World® Teddy Bear and Doll Convention. *A. Glenn Mandeville Collection.*

Love-CU is a breathtaking doll designed for the Collector's United Gathering, Atlanta, 1994. *A. Glenn Mandeville Collection.*

The Alexander Doll Company

1994 Special Dolls

America's Junior Miss 8" (20cm) –
Collector's United
Anne of Green Gables Trunk Set 8"
(20cm) – *Neiman Marcus*
Belle 8" (20cm) (Beauty and the Beast) –
Disney® License
Captain's Cruise 8" (20cm) – *Nashville Show FAD*
Caroline Travels the World Trunk Set 8" (20cm) – *Neiman Marcus*
Cinderella Gift Set 14" (36cm) "poor" dress – *Disney® Catalog*
Cinderella Gift Set 14" (36cm) Disney® print "poor" dress – *Disney® Catalog*
    (Note: doll not available until Summer, 1995)
Holly 8" (20cm) – *Belk & Leggett*
Joy 8" (20cm) – *Saks Fifth Avenue*
Little Huggums 12" 931cm) – *FAO Schwarz*
Little Miss Magnin Supports the Arts 8" (20cm) – *I. Magnin*
Little Women 8" (20cm) set of five dolls – *FAO Schwarz*
Love 8" (20cm) – *CU Gathering*
Maypole Dance 8" (20cm) – *Shirley's Doll House*
Navajo Woman 8" (20cm) – *MADC Convention*
Romeo and Juliet 21" (53cm) pair – *One-of-a-Kind, Disney® World Teddy Bear and Doll Convention Auction*
Secret Garden Trunk Set 8" (20cm) – *FAO Schwarz*
Setting Sail for Summer 8" (20cm) – *MADC Premiere*
Shadow of the Madame 8" (20cm) – *Doll and Teddy Bear Expo*
Sleeping Beauty Gift Set 14" (36cm) – *Disney® Catalog*
    (Note: advertised in 1994, but not shipped until 1995)
Tweedledee & Tweedledum 8" (20cm) pair – *Disney® World Teddy Bear and Doll Convention*
Wendy's Best Friend Maggie 8" (20cm) – *MADC Club Doll*
Wendy's Favorite Pastime 8" (20cm) – *Disney® License*
Wendy Starts Her Collection 8" (20cm) – *Jacobsen's*

Madame Alexander Doll Values

In this newly revised edition of *Alexander Dolls Value Guide*, you will note many changes, not only in pricing but in the number of listings. After the first edition, many generous collectors and dealers offered much primary resource material that resulted in a great many changes. Some dolls were on the market longer than was originally noted; others had several name changes. Some sizes were different and in some cases, dolls that were believed to be Alexander doll creations were deleted because of a lack of substantial proof of origin.

As in the first edition, I have made every attempt not to include a doll unless I personally had either seen the doll or a photograph of it with original advertising bearing its correct name. The name collectors assign a doll is not always the one given by the company.

At this time there is not documented proof that many of the celebrity dolls attributed to The Alexander Doll Company are not just beautiful and rare dolls with names like "Pink Champagne", but made with the same great care and expense. Because many of these dolls are so exquisite and almost impossible to find in mint condition, the values, in my opinion, are not affected. A rose by any other name smells just as sweet!

Many people will ask why some doll values have dropped substantially and others have risen by over $1,000 since the first edition. The accurate prices in this edition are based on comparing collector and dealer sales in this edition to those in the last edition. It is not enough to see a doll advertised for a certain price. The price I chose to list was the actual selling price. One can ask anything for a doll, but not find a buyer. Prices that assist the reader of this book, must be based on proven sales and not speculative pricing. The only exception to this is the occasional ultra rare doll which seldom comes up for sale. In that case, prices are based on what established collectors of this type of doll WOULD pay (often gladly) for

the chance to add this piece to a collection. Naturally, not every Alexander doll listed is bought or sold during a particular time frame, so prices reflect dolls similar in age, size or theme.

Another price changing factor was the celebration of several major dolls anniversaries last year, which drew attention away from what I call "classics" such as Alexander dolls. With this influence missing in 1995, I believe we will see substantial price increases in future editions. This is an excellent time to buy some of the lower priced dolls you have been wanting!

An additional catalyst is that The Alexander Doll Company, through their "Store Specials" and advertising from them, is gaining more visibility. Several annual collector events, besides the Madame Alexander Doll Club, now feature a limited edition exclusive doll for purchase. These dolls are rapidly escalating in value, especially among collectors who missed these events.

Finally, there is much interest in vintage Alexander dolls especially such dolls as *Scarlett* and the *Gone with the Wind Series*, *Little Women* and rare hard plastic rare dolls from the late 1940s and early 1950s. Another popular category is Dionne Quintuplet dolls. Mint dolls from any era are getting harder and harder to find, and often are sold privately for astronomical prices. Some of these collectors contacted me regarding privately purchased dolls thus allowing more information to be shared with the reader.

The indisputable beauty and artistry of Alexander Dolls is a tradition that will continue into the next century. Not only has The Alexander Doll Company been committed to the quality and appearance of their products, but they continue to incorporate innovative ideas and state of the art manufacturing techniques proving that a thing of beauty was, and ever shall be...a joy forever.

NOTE: Prices are based on excellent to mint dolls. An original box could add to value.

A very rare 8in (20cm) all composition *Little Colonel* doll with molded and painted hair. Her dress is tagged Little Colonel with the Little Colonel logo of a face in a ruffled collar. She dates from 1935. *Marge Meisinger Collection. Photograph by Michael Cadotte.*

ACTIVE MISS 18" (46cm)
hard plastic, 1954 ....$ 900.00

ADAMS, ABIGAIL 1st set,
First Ladies Series,
1976-1978........................120.00

ADAMS, LOUISA 1st set,
First Ladies Series,
1976-1978........................120.00

AFRICA 8" (20cm) hard
plastic, bend knee,
1966-1971....................275.00
8" (20cm) hard plastic,
straight legs, re-issued
1988-1992......................52.00

AGATHA 8" (20cm) hard
plastic, black top and
floral gown,
1953-1954....................980.00
18" (46cm) hard plastic,
pink taffeta, *Me and My
Shadow Series*,
1954 ....1,550.00
21" (53cm) *Portrait*, red
gown, 1967 ....550.00
10" (25cm) *Portrette*, red
velvet, 1968 ....420.00
21" (53cm) *Portrait*, rose
gown w/cape, 1974 .....375.00
21" (53cm) *Portrait*, blue
w/white sequin trim,
1975 ....265.00
21" (53cm) *Portrait*, blue
w/white rick-rack trim, 1976 ....265.00
21" (53cm) *Portrait*, lavender, 1979-1980 ....220.00
21" (53cm) *Portrait*, turquoise, 1981 ....220.00

AGNES cloth, 1930s 825.00

ALADDIN 8" (20cm) *Storyland Dolls*, 1993-1994 ....50.00

ALASKA 8" (20cm) *Americana Series*, 1990-1992 ....50.00

ALBANIA 8" (20cm) straight legs, 1987 ....90.00

ALCOTT, LOUISA MAY 14" (36cm) 1989-1990 ....85.00
8" (20cm) hard plastic, *Storyland Dolls*, 1992...55.00

ALEXANDER RAG TIME DOLLS cloth, 1938-1939 ....950.00

The *Little Colonel*, made in 1935, was Madame Alexander's version of the popular Ideal *Shirley Temple* doll. Both dolls had blonde ringlets, but the Alexander version had no dimples. She is all composition and is 13in (33cm) tall. *Marge Meisinger Collection. Photograph by Michael Cadotte.*

ALEXANDER-KINS 7-1/2-8" (19-20cm) hard plastic (sometimes called *Wendy, Wendy-Ann* or *Wendy-kins*).

Straight leg non-walker, 1953.

Coat, hat (dress).$475.00
Cotton dress, organdy pinafore, hat.....465.00
Cotton dress, cotton pinafore, hat.....465.00
Day in Country long gown....675.00-780.00
Easter doll (early version)....1,000.00 up
Felt jackets, pleated dresses.............575.00
Garden Party gown...............700.00
Jumper, bodysuit..400.00
Nightgown...........400.00
Nude, perfect doll...................375.00
Organdy dress, pinafore, hat....................425.00
Robe or P.J.s........225.00
Satin dress, pinafore, hat....................425.00
Sleeveless pinafore 350.00
Taffeta dress, cotton pinafore, hat 450.00

Straight leg walker, 1955.

Basic doll in box, panties, shoes, socks 425.00
Coat, hat...375.00
Cotton dress, pinafore, hat...375.00
Cotton school dress 265.00
Day in the Country 675.00
Garden Party long gown...560.00
Maypole Dance...670.00

31

No, this is not an Ideal *Shirley Temple* doll, but Madame Alexander's 1935 *Little Colonel* doll, based on the public domain book and not the movie. It was the kind of marketing strategy Madame Alexander was known for. The doll is 18in (46cm) tall, all composition with sleep eyes and a blonde mohair wig in curls. The doll did NOT feature dimples, and thus represented a literary character. *Alexander Doll Company. Photograph Courtesy of Bob Gantz.*

ALEXANDER-KINS
continued

Nightgown....$165.00
Nude, perfect
    doll..............350.00
Organdy dress,
    hat...............400.00
P.J.s.................175.00
Riding habit.....300.00
Robe, P.J.s........185.00
Sailor dress......575.00
Sleeveless organdy
    dress.............285.00
Swimsuits.........245.00
Taffeta party dress,
    hat................425.00

Bend knee walker, 1956-1964.

Basic doll in box, panties, shoes, socks	300.00
Carcoat	385.00
Cherry Twin	950.00 up
Coat, hat (dress)	325.00
Cotton dress, pinafore, hat	360.00
Cotton or satin dress, pinafore, hat	360.00
Felt jacket, pleated skirt, dress, hat	450.00
First dancing dress	465.00
Flower girl	775.00 up
June Wedding	625.00
Long party dress	700.00
Neiman Marcus doll in case, all clothes	1,200.00 up
Nightgown, robe	220.00
Nude	200.00
Organdy dress, organdy pinafore, hat	395.00
Riding habit, boy	395.00

The mold over which the cloth faces of the *Little Shavers* dolls in the 1930s and 1940s were pressed was found at the Alexander Doll Company. *Alexander Doll Company. Photograph courtesy of Bob Gantz.*

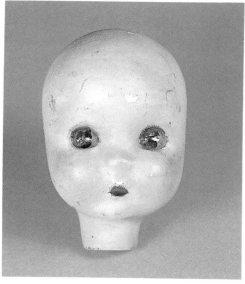

ALEXANDER-KINS
continued

Riding habit, corduroy,
    girl................................$ 400.00
Skater.......................................265.00
Sleeveless school dress..........260.00
Sundress..................................265.00
Swimsuits, beach outfits........260.00
Taffeta dress, hat....................370.00
Velvet party dress 380.00

Bend knee, non-walkers, 1965-1972.
Basic doll w/panties, shoes, socks 195.00
Cotton dress, 1965...165.00
Easter doll..1,075.00 up
Felt jacket, skirt, dress, cap, hat, 1965...575.00
French braid, cotton dress, 1965 ....565.00
Nude, perfect doll..125.00
Organdy dress, hat, 1965...295.00
Riding habit, check pants, boy, 1965 ....365.00
Riding habit, check pants, girl, 1965 ....325.00
Sewing kit doll 1,100.00
ALGERIA 8" (20cm) straight leg, 1987-1988...................................85.00

From this basic mold, many composition characters were manufactured. This doll is called *Spanish* and was made from 1936-1940 in all composition with a mohair wig. The face was first used on the *Little Betty* dolls. *Marge Meisinger Collection. Photograph by Michael Cadotte.*

ALICE (SOMETIMES CALLED ALICE IN WONDERLAND)

16" (41cm) cloth, 1930s
..................$ 695.00 up
7" (18cm) composition,
1930s.....................375.00
9" (23cm) composition,
1930s.....................385.00
11-14" (28-36cm)
composition,
1936-1940..............485.00
13" (33cm) composition,
swivel waist,
1930s....................435.00
14-1/2–18" (37-46cm)
composition,
1948-1949...........550.00
21" (53cm) composition,
1948-1949...........1,025.00
14" (36cm) hard plastic,
1950.......................595.00
14-1/2" (37cm)
hard plastic,
1949-1950........675.00 up
14" (36cm) hard plastic
w/trousseau,
1951-1952.....1,600.00 up

17-23" (43-58cm) hard plastic, 1949-1950 ....800.00 up
18" (46cm) hard plastic, 1951 ....775.00 up
29" (74cm) cloth/vinyl, 1952..650.00
15" (38cm), 18" (46cm), 23" (58cm) hard plastic, 1951-1952 ....750.00 up
8" (20cm) hard plastic, 1955-1956..680.00 up
14" (36cm) plastic/vinyl, 1966-1992..90.00
8" (20cm) hard plastic, Disney Crest Color (Disneyland®,
    Disney World®), 1972-1976 *(see Special Dolls)* 475.00
8" (20cm) 1990-1992... 60.00
8" (20cm) red trim, 1993-1994 ....50.00

The *Dionne Quintuplets* dolls were made in many mediums. This is a 16in (41cm) all cloth doll with a hand painted face, made in 1936. Her dress is tagged Cecile. *Marge Meisinger Collection. Photograph by Michael Cadotte.*

ALICE AND THE JABBERWOCKY 12" (31cm) 1993 Disney World® Teddy Bear and Doll Convention, *(see Special Dolls)*.......$ 350.00

ALICE AND THE WHITE RABBIT 10" (25cm) made for Disney World®, 1991 *(see Special Dolls)*............335.00

ALL STAR 8" (20cm) white, *Americana Series*, minor costume change, 1994..55.00

8" (20cm) white or black, *Americana Series*, 1993...........................55.00

ALLISON 18" (46cm) cloth/vinyl, 1990-1991.....................................100.00

ALPINE CHRISTMAS TWINS 8" (20cm) made for Christmas Shoppe, 1992, *(see Special Dolls)* 165.00

ALTAR BOY 8" (20cm) hard plastic, *Americana Series*, 1991..............45.00

AMANDA 8" (20cm) hard plastic, *Americana Series*, 1961 ....1,250.00 up

AMERICAN BEAUTY 10" (25cm) *Portrette*, 1991-1992........................80.00

AMERICAN GIRL 7-8" (18-20cm) composition, 1938.........................400.00

9-11" (23-28cm) composition, 1937...450.00

8" (20cm) hard plastic, 1962-1963, called *McGuffey Ana* in 1964-1965 ....375.00

AMERICAN INDIAN 9" (23cm) composition, 1938-1939 ....335.00

AMERICAN TOTS 16-21" (41-53cm) cloth dressed in children's fashions 485.00

AMERICAN WOMEN'S VOLUNTEER SERVICE (AWVS) 14" (36cm) composition, 1942..825.00

AMISH BOY 8" (20cm) hard plastic, bend knee, *Americana Series*, 1966-1969 ....285.00

AMISH GIRL 8" (20cm) hard plastic, bend knee, *Americana Series,* 1966-1969 ....380.00

AMY *(see Little Women)*

The 1930s were the years of the celebrity children and their likenesses in doll form. From 1937 to 1939, the Alexander Doll Company issued a *Jane Withers* doll in all composition in several sizes. This mint 17in (43cm) version, has her original script pin with Jane Wither's signature. *Marge Meisinger Collection. Photograph by Michael Cadotte.*

ANASTASIA
  10" (25cm) *Portrette Series*, 1988-1989............$ 90.00
  14" (36cm) MADC Convention Special.......175.00

ANATOLIA
  8" (20cm) straight legs, 1987......................75.00

ANGEL
  8" (20cm) in pink, blue, white gowns, 1950s.................800.00 up
  8" (20cm) Guardian, 1954....................775.00 up
  8" (20cm) hard plastic, Baby, 1955........800.00 up

ANGEL FACE
  8" (20cm) made for Shirley's Doll House, 1990 *(see Special Dolls)*.........150.00

ANNA BALLERINA
  18" (46cm) composition, 1940........................825.00

ANNA KARENINA
  21" (53cm) *Portrait*, 1991..........................360.00

ANNABELLE
  14-15" (36-38cm) hard plastic, 1951-1952 ....535.00
  14-15" (36-38cm) trousseau/trunk, 1952..............................1,600.00
  18" (46cm) hard plastic, 1951-1952 ....685.00
  20-23" (51-58cm) hard plastic, 1951-1952 ....800.00
  29" (74cm) vinyl/cloth, 1952 *(Barbara Jane)*.............................675.00
  8" (20cm) made for Belk & Leggett, 1992 *(see Special Dolls)* 75.00

ANNE OF GREEN GABLES
  14" (36cm) Anne Goes to School, w/trunk, wardrobe, 1992-1993..........250.00
  14" (36cm) Anne's Trunk Set, w/trunk, wardrobe, 1994 ....250.00
  14 (36cm) Anne Arrives at Station, 1994 ....140.00
  14" (36cm) Anne Arrives at Station, 1992-1993 ....140.00
  14" (36cm) Anne Becomes the Teacher, 1993 ....125.00
    Puff sleeve dress, 1992...40.00
    White organdy dress, 1992 ....45.00
    Winter coat outfit, 1992..45.00
    Winter coat, 1994, minor costume change 45.00
  Anne's Puff Sleeve, 8" (20cm) hard plastic, 1994.............................60.00

McGuffey Ana is a character name that appears throughout Alexander doll history. This all composition doll is 15in (38cm) tall and was sold 1937-1944. While this doll came with a hat, the doll outfit illustrated on the wrist tag did not. *Marge Meisinger Collection. Photograph by Michael Cadotte.*

ANNETTE 14" (36cm) porcelain, 1993 *(see Special Dolls)*.....$ 450.00
ANNIE LAURIE 14" (36cm) composition, 1937...................625.00
17" (43cm) composition, 1937..925.00
ANTOINETTE 21" (53cm) composition, 1946.......................2,100.00
ANTONY, MARK 12" (31cm) *Portraits of History*, 1980-1985...............................75.00
APPLE ANNIE 8" (20cm) hard plastic, 1954.......................985.00 up
APPLE PIE 14" (36cm) *Classic Dolls*, 1991..............................85.00
APRIL 14" (36cm) *Classic Dolls*, 1990-1991..............................95.00
ARGENTINE BOY 8" (20cm) hard plastic, bend knee walker, 1965..500.00
8" (20cm) hard plastic, bend knee, 1965.....................400.00
ARGENTINE GIRL
8" (20cm) bend knee walker, 1965 ....200.00
8" (20cm) hard plastic, bend knee, 1965-1972 ....155.00
8" (20cm) hard plastic, straight legs, 1973-1976.....................75.00
8" (20cm) hard plastic, straight legs, 1976-1986.....................70.00
ARMENIA 8" (20cm) 1989-1990 ....50.00
ARRIVING IN AMERICA 8" (20cm) hard plastic, *Americana Series*, 1992-1993 ....55.00
ARTIE 12" (31cm) plastic/vinyl, made for FAO Schwarz, 1962..........325.00
ASHLEY 8" (20cm) jacket, hat, *Scarlett Series*, 1990.....................70.00
8" (20cm) hard plastic, Confederate Officer, *Scarlett Series*, 1991-1992........55.00
ASTROLOGICAL DOLLS OF THE MONTH 14-17" (36-43cm) composition, 1938 ....485.00
AUNT AGATHA 8" (20cm) hard plastic, 1957 ....985.00
AUNT BETSY cloth/felt, 1930s 925.00
AUNT PITTY PAT 14-17" (36-43cm) composition, 1939...................1,265.00 up
8" (20cm) hard plastic, 1957 ....1,575.00 up
8" (20cm) hard plastic, straight legs, *Scarlett Series*, 1991-1992........70.00
AUSTRALIA 8" (20cm) 1990-1991 ....55.00
AUSTRIA 8" (20cm) hard plastic, *International Series*, 1994 ....50.00
AUSTRIA BOY* Straight legs, 1973-1975..........................80.00
1976-1989 ....75.00
AUSTRIA GIRL* Straight legs, 1973-1975..........................80.00
1976-1990 ....65.00
*Formerly Tyrolean Boy and Girl

AUTUMN
14" (36cm)
Classic Dolls,
1993........$135.00
AUTUMN LEAVES
14" (36cm)
Classic Dolls,
1994.........120.00
AUTUMN IN N.Y.
10" (25cm)
made for First
Modern Doll
Club, 1991 *(see
Special Dolls)*
.................225.00

AVRIL, JANE 10" (25cm) made for Marshall Fields, 1989, *(see Special Dolls)*..195.00

B

BABBIE cloth, inspired by Katherine Hepburn............................$2,225.00
BABETTE 10" (25cm) *Portrette Series*, 1988-1989 ....95.00
BABS SKATER 18" (46cm) composition......................................700.00
15" (38cm) hard plastic, 1948-1950 ....725.00
17-18" (43-46cm) hard plastic...775.00
21" (53cm) hard plastic ....850.00 up
BABY BETTY 10-12" (25-31cm) composition, 1935-1936..............280.00
BABY BROTHER AND SISTER 20" (51cm) cloth/vinyl, 1977-1979.....100.00 each
14" (36cm) 1979-1982..90.00 each
14" (36cm) re-introduced 1989..70.00 each
BABY CLOWN 8" (20cm) hard plastic, painted face, 1955............1,250.00 up
BABY ELLEN 14" (36cm) 1965-1972....................................145.00
BABY GENIUS 11" (28cm) all cloth, 1930s..............................500.00
11-12" (28-31cm) composition/cloth, 1930s-1940s 200.00
16" (41cm) composition/cloth, 1930s-1940s.............................200.00
15" (38cm) hard plastic head/vinyl limbs, 1949-1950..................185.00
18" (46cm) hard plastic head/vinyl limbs, 1949-1950..................295.00
21" (53cm) hard plastic head/vinyl limbs, 1949-1950..................385.00
8" (20cm) hard plastic/vinyl, 1956-1962 *(see Little Genius)*
BABY JANE 16" (41cm) composition, 1935 ....900.00 up
BABY LYNN 20" (51cm) cloth/vinyl, 1973-1976...........................135.00
BABY MCGUFFEY 22-24" (56-61cm) composition, 1937 ....360.00
20" (51cm) cloth/vinyl, 1971-1976 ....245.00
14" (36cm) cloth/vinyl, 1972-1978 ....185.00

America's obsession with the Dionne Quintuplets is visible in Madame's set of 8in (20cm) all composition *Dionne Quints*, and a 14in (36cm) composition *Dr. DeFoe*, available 1937-1939. The contract with the Quintuplet Guardians enabled the Alexander Doll Company to become an industry leader. *Marge Meisinger Collection. Photograph by Michael Cadotte.*

BABY PRECIOUS

14" (36cm) cloth/vinyl, 1975....................$ 100.00

21" (53cm) cloth/vinyl, 1974-discontinued 1976.......................125.00

BAD LITTLE GIRL

16" (41cm) cloth, blue dress, companion to *Good Little Girl*, 1966......125.00

BALI 8" (20cm) *International Dolls*, 1993....50.00

BALLERINA *(also see individual dolls)*

9" (23cm) composition, 1935-1941...............350.00

11-14" (28-36cm) composition, 1936-1938...............450.00

17" (43cm) composition, 1938-1941...............565.00

21" (53cm) hard plastic, *Deborah Ballerina*, 1947.....................3,050.00

15-18" (38-46cm) hard plastic, 1950-1952..585.00

8" (20cm) hard plastic straight leg non-walker, lavender, yellow, pink, 1953.........................800.00

blue (rare)...925.00

8" (20cm) hard plastic, straight leg walker, lavender, yellow, pink, blue, 1954-1955 ....535.00

8" (20cm) white, 1955 ....575.00

8" (20cm) rose, 1956 ....575.00

8" (20cm) yellow, 1956 ....500.00

15" (38cm) hard plastic, *Binnie*, 1956..325.00

18" (46cm) hard plastic, *Binnie*, 1956..400.00

10" (25cm) hard plastic, 1957-1959 ....445.00

12" (31cm) hard plastic, *Lissy*, 1956, 1958 ....475.00

16-1/2" (42cm) *Elise Ballerina*, jointed at ankle, knee, hip, elbow and shoulder, 1957-1964..385.00

16-1/2" (42cm) hard plastic, 1957..390.00

BALLERINA *continued*

16-1/2" (42cm) hard plastic, white tutu, 1958................$ 375.00

16-1/2" (42cm) hard plastic, gold tutu and slippers, 1959......380.00

16-1/2" (42cm) hard plastic, pink tutu, 1960....................365.00

16-1/2" (42cm) hard plastic, pink tutu (upswept hairdo), 1961....................375.00

16-1/2" (42cm) hard plastic, blue tutu, 1962....................365.00

16-1/2" (42cm), blue tutu, variation of face and hair piece: wreath of small flowers (1963), large flowers (1964), 1963-1964...........400.00

8" (20cm) bend knee walker, 1957-1965..485.00

8" (20cm) blue, 1957 ....425.00

8" (20cm) pink, 1958 ....385.00

8" (20cm) gold, 1959 ....475.00

8" (20cm) lavender, 1961..585.00

8" (20cm) bend knee, yellow, 1965-1972 ....395.00

8" (20cm) blue, 1962-1972..255.00

8" (20cm) pink, 1962-1972..235.00

14" (36cm) 1965...425.00

17" (43cm) plastic/vinyl, discontinued costume, 1967-1989 ....145.00

17" (43cm) 1970-1971 ....355.00

14" (36cm) plastic/vinyl, 1973-1982 ....195.00

8" (20cm) straight legs, 1973-1992 (1985-1987 white face).....................80.00

8" (20cm) ballerina trunk set, made for Enchanted Doll House, 1983 *(see Special Dolls)* 175.00

8" (20cm) Ballerina, MADC, 1984 *(see Special Dolls)* 250.00

8" (20cm) made for Enchanted Doll House, 1989 *(see Special Dolls)* 85.00

12" (31cm) *Muffin*, 1989-1990 ....70.00

12" (31cm) *Romance Collection*, 1990-1992 ....72.00

Everyone loved Scarlett O'Hara, and so did Madame Alexander. This 1939-1940 *Scarlett O'Hara* is mint in her original box, with the rare wrist tag. She is 18in (46cm) tall, all composition with sleep eyes. *Marge Meisinger Collection. Photograph by Michael Cadotte.*

BALLERINA *continued*
8" (20cm) white/gold, *Americana Series*, 1990-1991, black or white dolls......$ 65.00
   pink, white only, 1993-1994........47.00
   pink, black or white doll, 1992.........55.00
17" (43cm) plastic/ vinyl, *Firebird* and *Swan Lake*, 1990-1991..........125.00
12" (31cm) Ballerina, 1993 *(Classic Lissy)* 95.00
21" (53cm) vinyl, *Lilac Fairie Ballerina*, 1993-1994 (vinyl *Cissy*)................300.00

BARBARA JANE
  29" (74cm) cloth/vinyl, 1952 ....465.00
BARBARY COAST   10" (25cm) hard plastic, *Portrette Series*, 1962-1963...1,260.00
BARTON, CLARA   10" (25cm) *Portrette Series*, 1989...................................95.00
BATHING BEAUTY   10" (25cm) UFDC Special Doll, 1992 *(see Special Dolls)*...300.00
BEAST   8" (20cm) hard plastic, *Storyland Dolls*, 1994 ....55.00
  12" (31cm) *Romance Series*, 1992...125.00
BEAUX ART DOLLS   18" (46cm) hard plastic, 1953.......................1,550.00
BEAU BRUMMEL   cloth, 1930s..785.00
BEAUTY   8" (20cm) hard plastic, *Storyland Dolls*, 1994...............................60.00
  12" (31cm) *Romance Series*, 1992...105.00
BEAUTY QUEEN   10" (25cm) hard plastic, 1961 *(see Cissette)*....................285.00
BEDDY-BYE BROOKE   14" (36cm) made for FAO Schwarz, 1991 *(see Special Dolls)*...90.00
BEDDY-BYE BROOKE & BRENDA   14" (36cm) and 8" (20cm), made for FAO Schwarz, 1992 *(see Special Dolls)* 175.00
BELGIUM   7" (18cm) composition, 1935-1938..355.00
  8" (20cm) hard plastic, bend knee, 1972 ....125.00
  8" (20cm) straight legs, 1973-1975...80.00
  8" (20cm) straight legs, 1976-1988...70.00
BELLE OF THE BALL   10" (25cm) *Portrette Series*, 1989..............................85.00

Composition dolls, while somewhat fragile, were a great love of Madame Alexander. This 18in (46cm) *Fairy Princess* has sleep eyes and a mohair wig. She was made from 1939-1943. *Marge Meisinger Collection. Photograph by Michael Cadotte.*

BELLE WATLING
10" (25cm) *Scarlett Series*, 1992......$ 90.00
BELLOWS' ANNE
14" (36cm) plastic/ vinyl, *Fine Arts Series*, 1987........100.00
BERNHARDT, SARAH
21" (53cm) dressed in all burgundy, 1987.....................300.00
BESSY BELL
14" (36cm) plastic/ vinyl, *Classic Dolls*, 1988......................85.00
BESSY BROOKS
8" (20cm) *Storyland Dolls*, 1988-1991 ....70.00

BESSY BROOKS BRIDE   8" (20cm), Greenville Show, 1990
(see Special Dolls)..80.00
BEST MAN   8" (20cm) hard plastic, 1955 ....700.00
BETH   *(see Little Women)*
BETH   10" (25cm) made for Spiegel, 1990 *(see Special Dolls)*.................105.00
BETTY   12" (31cm) composition, 1936-1937 ....475.00
16" (36cm) composition, 1935-1942.....................................350.00
16-18" (41-46cm) composition, 1935-1942...........................400.00
19-21" (48-53cm) composition, 1938-1941 ....400.00
14-1/2–17-1/2" (37-45cm) hard plastic, made for Sears in 1951 ....525.00
30" (76cm) plastic/vinyl, 1960..420.00
BETTY, LITTLE   9" (23cm) composition, 1935-1943 ....325.00
BETTY, TINY   7" (18cm) composition, 1934-1943...............................355.00
BETTY BAG   all cloth, flat painted face, yarn hair, 1940s.....................335.00
BETTY BLUE   8" (20cm) straight legs, Storyland Dolls,
1987-1988 only..75.00
BIBLE CHARACTER DOLLS   8" (20cm) hard plastic, 1954.................6,100.00
BILL   8" (20cm) hard plastic, 1955-1963 ....585.00
Groom, 1953-1957..565.00

This all composition *Madelaine* was a deluxe version with a human hair wig in a 14in (36cm) size. She was manufactured in 1940. *Marge Meisinger Collection. Photograph by Michael Cadotte.*

BINNIE WALKER
   15-18" (38-46cm)
   hard plastic,
   1954-1955
   .....$155.00-285.00
   15" (38cm) in
   trunks, wardrobe
   ....985.00
   15" (38cm) Skater,
   hard plastic,
   1955..........650.00
   18" (46cm)
   Toddler, plastic/
   vinyl, 1964
   ....350.00 up
   25" (64cm) hard plastic, 1954-1955.................................475.00
   25" (64cm) in formals, 1955.................................495.00 up
BIRTHDAY, HAPPY MADC, 1985 *(see Special Dolls)* 395.00
BIRTHDAY DOLLS 7" (18cm) composition 345.00
BITSEY 11-12" (28-31cm) composition, 1942-1946 ....275.00
   11-16" (28-41cm) head hard plastic, 1949-1951 ....175.00
   12" (31cm) cloth/vinyl, 1965-1966.................................155.00
   19-26" (48-66cm) 1949-1951 ....200.00-265.00
BITSEY, LITTLE 9" (23cm) all vinyl, 1967-1968...............125.00
   11-16" (28-41cm)...55.00-200.00
BLACK FOREST 8" (20cm) 1989-1990.................................65.00
BLISS, BETTY TAYLOR 2nd set, *First Ladies Series*, 1979-1981 ....135.00
BLUE BOY 7" (18cm) composition, 1936-1938.................375.00
   9" (23cm) composition, 1938-1941 ....400.00
   12" (31cm) plastic/vinyl, *Portrait Children*, 1972-1983 ....95.00
   In blue velvet, 1985-1987 ....125.00
BLUE DANUBE WALTZ 18" (46cm) hard plastic, blue taffeta,
   Me and My Shadow Series, 1954.................................1,275.00 up
BLUE FAIRIE 10" (25cm) *Portrette Series*, 1993-1994..........85.00

Sonja Henie was the richest woman in the world in the 1930s. As a result, she asked for an exclusive head mold for a doll in her likeness. This all composition doll dates from 1939-1942 and has a human hair wig. Deluxe versions were available in gift boxes with wardrobes. *Marge Meisinger Collection. Photograph by Michael Cadotte.*

BLUE MOON
14" (36cm)
Classic Dolls,
1991-1992.....$170.00
BLUE ZIRCON
10" (25cm)
Birthday Collection,
1992 ....64.00
BO PEEP, LITTLE
7" (18cm) composition,
Storyland Dolls,
1937-1941....355.00
9-11" (23-28cm)
composition,
1936-1940....360.00
7-1/2" (19cm) hard
plastic, straight leg
walker, 1955 470.00
8" (20cm) hard plastic,
bend knee walker,
1962-1964....395.00
8" (20cm) hard plastic,
bend knee,
1965-1972....155.00
8" (20cm) hard plastic,
straight legs,
1973-1975......75.00
8" (20cm) hard plastic,
1976-1987......75.00
10" (25cm) *Portrette*,
1994 ....75.00

14" (36cm) *Classic Dolls*, 1988-1989 ....75.00
12" (31cm) porcelain, 1990-1992...255.00
14" (36cm) re-introduced 1992-1993 ....132.00
BOBBIE SOX   8" (20cm) hard plastic, made for Disney World®, 1990
(see Special Dolls) 110.00
BOBBY   8" (20cm) hard plastic, 1957...............................485.00
8" (20cm) hard plastic, 1960 ....525.00
BOBBY Q.   cloth, 1940-1942..650.00 up
BOBO CLOWN   8" (20cm) 1991-1992..52.00

44

These delightful 9in (23cm) all composition dolls are called *Rumbero* and *Rumbera*, and date from 1941. *Marge Meisinger Collection. Photograph by Michael Cadotte.*

BOHEMIA 8" (20cm) 1989-1991..$ 50.00
BOLIVIA
   8" (20cm) hard plastic, bend knee and bend knee walker, 1963-1966 ....300.00 up
BON VOYAGE LITTLE MISS MAGNIN
   8" (20cm) made for I. Magnin, 1993 *(see Special Dolls)* 95.00
BON VOYAGE MISS MAGNIN
   10" (25cm), made for I. Magnin, 1993 *(see Special Dolls)* 135.00
BONNIE (BABY)
   16-19" (41-48cm) vinyl, 1954-1955 ....95.00
   24-30" (61-76cm) 1954-1955 ....190.00
BONNIE BLUE #1305, 14" (36cm) *Jubilee II*, 1989 ....120.00
   8" (20cm) hard plastic, 1990-1992 ....60.00
BONNIE GOES TO LONDON 8" (20cm) *Scarlett Series*, 1993-1994 ....75.00
BONNIE TODDLER 18" (46cm) cloth/hard plastic head, vinyl limbs,
   1950-1951
   ....130.00
   19" (48cm) all vinyl, 1954-1955..155.00
BOONE, DANIEL 8" (20cm) hard plastic, *Americana Series*, 1991 ....60.00
BRAZIL 7" (18cm) composition, 1937-1943 ....345.00

The name *Little Genius* was a favorite that would be used several times. It still is used today. This version dates from 1942-1946 and is 12in (31cm) tall with composition head and hands and a cloth body. *Marge Meisinger Collection. Photograph by Michael Cadotte.*

BRAZIL *continued*
   9" (23cm) composition,
     1938-1940...$ 275.00
   8" (20cm) hard plastic,
     bend knee walker,
     1965-1972 .....195.00
     bend knee 120.00
   8" (20cm) hard plastic,
     straight legs,
     1973-1975 ....75.00
   8" (20cm) hard plastic,
     straight legs,
     1976-1988 ....65.00
   1985-1987
     white face.....60.00

BRENDA STARR
   12" (31cm) hard plastic/
     vinyl, 1964 ....240.00
   Ball gown 275.00

Beach outfit..195.00
Bride 325.00
Raincoat, hat, dress..265.00
Street dresses 190.00

BRIAR ROSE 8" (20cm) MADC, 1989 *(see Special Dolls)*................350.00

BRIDE 7" (18cm) composition, 1935-1939.............................. 275.00
   9-11" (23-28cm) composition, 1936-1941 ....350.00
   13" (33cm), 14" (36cm), 15" (38cm) composition, 1935-1941.......300.00
   17-18" (43-46cm) composition, 1935-1943 ....425.00
   21" (53cm) composition, *Royal Wedding Portrait*, 1945-1947 ....2,100.00 up
   21-22" (53-56cm) composition, 1942-1943 ....600.00
     In trunk, trousseau, composition ....1,600.00 up
   14" (36cm) Pink Bride, 1950 ....775.00
   18" (46cm) Pink Bride, 1950................................825.00-950.00
   23" (58cm) hard plastic 1949, 1952-1955.........................695.00
   8" (20cm) hard plastic, *Quizkin*, 1953 ....675.00 up
   8" (20cm) hard plastic, 1955-1958...................................345.00
   25" (64cm) hard plastic, 1995 ....725.00
   10" (25cm) hard plastic, in trunk, trousseau, 1950s.............950.00 up
   18" (46cm) hard plastic, 1949-1955..................................695.00
   21" (53cm) hard plastic, 1949-1953..................................900.00
   15" (38cm) hard plastic, 1951-1955..................................600.00
   8" (20cm) hard plastic/bend knee walker, 1963....................250.00
   8" (20cm) hard plastic/bend knee walker in ruffled dress, 1964-1965 ..350.00

During the walking doll craze, the Alexander Doll Company created this great doll, called *Jeannie Walker*, in an all composition medium. This version is stock number 1600 and dates from 1942. *Marge Meisinger Collection. Photograph by Michael Cadotte.*

Cissy Brides

Lucille Ball *Forever Darling* Bride - Lace over-skirt with pleated underskirt, elaborate cap bridal veil decorated with flowers.
    (This doll was made the same year as the film *Forever Darling* with Lucille Ball and Desi Arnez.)
    1955.............$3,100.00 up
Brocade gown appliqued bodice and skirt, *A Child's Dream Come True Series,* 1955..................500.00
Gown has lace bodice, tulle skirt finely pleated tulle Cap with veil, *Cissy Fashion Parade Series,* 1956........500.00
Gown white satin bodice, double train, tulle skirt, *Cissy Models Her Formal Gowns Series,* 1957................................535.00
Gown of fragile lace bridal, wreath pattern at bottom of skirt, *Dolls to Remember Series,* 1958....................................600.00
21" (53cm) doll has straight arms and short neck. Gown of nylon pleated tulle, puffed sleeves, 1959......................................550.00
21" (53cm) doll has straight arms and short neck. Gown beige lace overskirt, pleated tulle underskirt, 1962 ....625.00
21" (53cm) porcelain, 1994..500.00

Ready to serve her country, this all composition WAAC doll is 14in (36cm) tall with a mohair wig and metal insignias. She was manufactured in 1943-1944 to help stimulate patriotism in young children. *Marge Meisinger Collection. Photograph by Michael Cadotte.*

Cissette Brides

10" (25cm) hard plastic, gown tulle w/short veil (pictured on front cover of *Madame Alexander presents Cissette* - promotion book that came with early dolls), 1957..................$ 300.00

10" (25cm) hard plastic, gown tulle and bridal lace w/tulle cap veil. (matches *Cissy* 1956 and *Lissy* 1957 Brides), 1957 ....300.00

10" (25cm) hard plastic, gown lace bridal wreath pattern. (matches *Cissy* and *Elise* brides of same year), 1958.............325.00

10" (25cm) hard plastic, gown tulle w/puffed sleeves, 1959-1960..............300.00

10" (25cm) hard plastic, gown tulle w/rhinestones on collar and veil, 1961 ....300.00

10" (25cm) hard plastic, gown has lace on bodice and lacetrim on skirt, long veil, 1962..........300.00

10" (25cm) hard plastic, gown tulle w/rows of lace at bodice and hem of skirt (matches *Elise* bride of same year), 1963........................300.00

Lissy Brides

12" (31cm) doll jointed at arms, elbow, knee, hip and shoulder. Gown tulle w/tulle cap veil, 1956 ....275.00

12" (31cm) same doll (jointed) and gown as 1956 but w/long veil, 1957 ....275.00

12" (31cm) jointed doll. Gown dotted net, w/tulle veil, 1958 ....275.00

The 21in (53cm) all composition *Margaret O'Brien* doll, available in 1946-1947 is a collector's dream. Mint dolls like this are very hard to find. *Marge Meisinger Collection. Photograph by Michael Cadotte.*

Elise Brides, dolls were jointed at ankle, knee, hip, elbow and shoulder, 1957-1964
  16-1/2" (42cm) hard plastic, gown nylon tulle, chapel length veil, 1957......$ 345.00
  16-1/2" (42cm) hard plastic, gown tulle bridal wreath pattern on skirt, 1958...375.00
  16-1/2" (42cm) hard plastic, gown tulle w/puffed sleeves, long veil, 1959..............................350.00
  16-1/2" (42cm) hard plastic, gown satin, bodice has a lace bertha decorated w/sequins and crystal beads, 1960...................335.00
  16-1/2" (42cm) hard plastic, gown tulle w/puffed sleeves. Doll has short hair style, 1961.............325.00
  16-1/2" (42cm) hard plastic, gown "cobwebby" pattern lace on bodice and trim of tulle skirt, 1962.............325.00
  18" (46cm) vinyl, gown tulle rows of lace at bodice and hem. Jacqueline hairstyle w/spit curl (various hair colors), 1963................375.00
  18" (46cm) hard plastic/vinyl, gown white lace bodice and sleeves, tiers of lace on skirt, chapel length veil, white satin ribbon bow at waist, 1964...345.00
  8" (20cm) hard plastic, 1960 ....350.00
  8" (20cm) bend knee walker, 1963-1965 ....285.00
  21" (53cm) *Portrait*, full lace, lace edge on veil, 1965 ....945.00
  8" (20cm) bend knee, 1966-1972 ....175.00
  17" (43cm) plastic/vinyl, 1965-1970...325.00
  17" (43cm) plastic/vinyl, 1966-1971...275.00
  17" (43cm) plastic/vinyl, 1966-1988...150.00
  21" (53cm) full lace overskirt, plain veil, 1969 ....800.00
  8" (20cm) straight legs, 1973-1975 ....80.00

Madame Alexander loved the British Royal Family. This 21in (53cm) all composition *Princess Margaret Rose* has a human hair wig and her clover wrist tag. She was manufactured in 1946-1947. *Marge Meisinger Collection. Photograph by Michael Cadotte.*

Elise Brides *continued*
14" (36cm) plastic/vinyl,
   1973-1976 ....$ 100.00
8" (20cm) straight legs,
   1976-1992...............55.00
8" (20cm) white face,
   1985-1987...............60.00
14" (36cm) plastic/vinyl,
   Classic Dolls,
   1987-1990.............110.00
21" (53cm) porcelain,
   1989-1990.............510.00
10" (25cm) *Portrette Series*,
   1990-1991.............100.00
12" (31cm) porcelain,
   1991-1993.............255.00
14" (36cm) ecru gown,
   re-introduced
   1992 ....180.00
8" (20cm) Bride,
   Americana Series,
   1990-1994...............70.00

BRIDESMAID
9" (23cm) composition,
   1937-1939..............355.00
11-14" (28-36cm) compo-
   sition, 1938-1942..370.00
15-18" (38-46cm) compo-
   sition, 1939-1944..395.00

20-22" (51-56cm) composition, *Portrait*, 1941-1947 ....1,535.00
21-1/2" (55cm) composition, 1938-1941 ....985.00
15-17" (38-43cm) hard plastic, 1950-1952 ....600.00
18" (46cm) hard plastic, 1952 ....625.00
19" (48cm) rigid vinyl, in pink, 1952-1953 ....575.00
15" (38cm) hard plastic, 1952 ....450.00
15" (38cm) hard plastic, 1955 ....300.00
18" (46cm) hard plastic, 1955 .... 400.00
25" (64cm) hard plastic, 1955 ....525.00
8" (20cm) hard plastic, straight leg walker, 1955 ....565.00
20" (51cm) hard plastic, 1956 ....565.00
8" (20cm) bend knee walker, 1956..675.00
8" (20cm) bend knee walker, 1957-1958 ....665.00

Fairy Queen is a 14in (36cm) all hard plastic doll, completely mint and original with her clover wrist tag. She dates from 1948-1950. *Marge Meisinger Collection. Photograph by Michael Cadotte.*

Elise Brides *continued*
16-1/2" (42cm)
hard plastic,
1957-1959.......$ 445.00
10" (25cm)
hard plastic,
1957-1963........475.00
12" (31cm)
hard plastic,
1956-1959.........455.00
17" (43cm)
plastic/vinyl,
1966-1971 ....275.00

BRIGITTA
11" (28cm) & 14" (36cm), *(see Sound of Music)*

BRINKER, GRETEL
12" (31cm) 1993 ....90.00

BRINKER, HANS
12" (31cm) 1993 ....90.00

BROOKE
14" (36cm) made for FAO Schwarz, 1988 *(see Special Dolls)*.........120.00

BUBBLES CLOWN
8" (20cm), *Americana Series*, 1993-1994 ....50.00

BUCK RABBIT
cloth/felt, 1930s...625.00

BUD
16-19" (41-48cm) cloth/vinyl, 1952 ....175.00
19" & 25" (48cm & 64cm) 1952-1953..265.00

BULGARIA
8" (20cm) 1985-1987..65.00

BUMBLE BEE   8" (20cm) hard plastic, *Americana Series*, 1992-1993...50.00
BUNNY   18" (46cm) plastic/vinyl, 1962 ....270.00
BURMA   7" (18cm) composition, 1939-1943 ....345.00
BUTCH   14-16" (36-41cm) composition/cloth, 1949-1951 ....165.00
11-12" (28-31cm) composition/cloth, 1942-1946 ....160.00
11-16" (28-41cm) hard plastic, 1949-1951......................................160.00 up
14" (36cm) cloth/vinyl head and limbs, 1950 ....140.00
12" (31cm) cloth/vinyl, 1965-1966 ....90.00
BUTCH , LITTLE   9" (23cm) all vinyl, 1967-1968...........................140.00
BUTCH McGUFFEY   22" (56cm) composition/cloth, 1940-1941 ....225.00

51

An outstanding doll is this *Nina Ballerina*, made in all hard plastic and illustrated here in a 15in (38cm) size. Available in 1951, she is a very sought after doll because of her embroidery floss wig. *Marge Meisinger Collection. Photograph by Michael Cadotte*

CALAMITY JANE 8" (20cm) hard plastic, *Americana Series*, 1994..$ 50.00

CAMELOT IN COLUMBIA 8" (20cm) made for Columbia Show, 1991 *(see Special Dolls)*..100.00

CAMEO LADY 10" (25cm) CU, 1991 *(see Special Dolls)* 125.00

CAMILLE 21" (53cm) composition, 1938-1939....2,000.00 up

CANADA 8" (20cm) hard plastic, bend knee, 1968-1972....125.00 straight legs, 1973-1975......75.00 straight legs, 1976-1988......65.00 white face, 1986 ..65.00

CAPTAIN HOOK 8" (20cm) hard plastic, 1992-1993.........65.00

CAREEN 8" (20cm) *Scarlett Series*, 1994 ...55.00 14" (36cm) plastic/vinyl, *Scarlett Series*, 1992-1993....125.00

CARMEN

7" (18cm) composition, 1938-1943 ....345.00
9-11" (23-28cm) composition, boy and girl, 1938-1943................325.00 each
11" (28cm) composition, sleep eyes, 1937-1939......................370.00
11-13" (28-33cm) composition, 1937-1940 ....495.00
15-18" (38-46cm) composition, 1939-1942 ....695.00
21" (53cm) composition, 1939-1942...1,035.00
14" (36cm) plastic/vinyl, *Opera Series*, 1983-1986 ....110.00
CARMEN MIRANDA PORTRETTE 1993...75.00
CARNIVAL IN RIO 21" (53cm) porcelain, 1989-1990 ....460.00
CARNIVAL IN VENICE 21" (53cm) porcelain, 1990-1991 ....525.00

Louisa May Alcott's endearing tale, *Little Men*, inspired a series of three 15in (38cm) hard plastic characters from the novel. Here is *Tommy Bangs*, in mint condition, with his clover wrist tag. He was manufactured in 1952. *Marge Meisinger Collection. Photograph by Michael Cadotte.*

CARNIVALLE DOLL
  14" (36cm) made for
  FAO Schwarz, 1991
  (see Special Dolls)..$ 210.00
CAROLINE 15" (38cm)
  vinyl, in dresses, pants,
    1961-1962...............300.00
  In boy hairstyle
    (possibly *John Jr.*),
    undressed...............475.00
  In riding habit............365.00
  In case/wardrobe..1,450.00 up

CAROLINE 8" (20cm) made for Belk & Leggett, 1993
  (see Special Dolls) 80.00
  8" (20cm) Caroline Loves Storyland, Neiman Marcus, 1993..........250.00
CARREEN 14-17" (36-43cm) composition, 1937-1938 ....950.00
  8" (20cm) hard plastic, *Scarlett Series,* 1994.....................55.00
CARROT TOP 21" (53cm) cloth, 1967 ....140.00
CENTURY OF FASHIONS 14" & 18" (36 & 46cm) hard plastic,
  1954 ....1,530.00
CHARITY 8" (20cm) hard plastic, *Americana Series*, 1961 ....1,225.00
CHARLENE 18" (46cm) cloth/vinyl, 1991-1992...............................105.00
CHATTERBOX 24" (61cm) plastic/vinyl, talker, 1961 ....270.00
CHEERLEADER 8" (20cm) made for I. Magnin, 1990
  (see Special Dolls) 75.00
  8" (20cm) hard plastic, black or white doll, royal blue, gold outfit,
    Americana Series, 1992 ....52.00
  8" (20cm) *Americana Series*, 1990-1993 ....55.00
CHERI 18" (46cm) hard plastic, white satin gown, pink opera coat,
  Me and My Shadow Series, 1954 ....1,335.00
CHERRY TWINS 8" (20cm) hard plastic, 1957 only ....900.00 up each
CHERUB 12" (31cm) vinyl, 1960-1961 ....482.00
  18" (46cm) hard plastic head, cloth/vinyl, early 1950s 370.00
CHERUB BABIES cloth, 1930s 490.00
CHILE 8" (20cm) hard plastic, 1992...62.00
CHINA 7" (18cm) composition, 1936-1940 ....265.00
  9" (23cm) composition, 1935-1938..272.00

This 15in (38cm) all hard plastic doll is *Nat*, from the 1952 series of Little Men. These dolls are very popular with collectors. *Marge Meisinger Collection. Photograph by Michael Cadotte.*

CHINA *continued*
   8" (20cm) hard plastic,
      bend knee, 1972
      ....$ 110.00
   8" (20cm) Smiling
      face......................137.00
   Straight legs,
      1973-1975..............72.00
   Straight legs,
      1976-1986..............65.00
      1987-1989..............62.00
CHRISTENING BABY
   11-13" (28-33cm) cloth/
      vinyl, 1951-1954...89.00
   16-19" (41-48cm)...120.00
CHRISTINE 21" (53cm)
   one-of-a-kind, Disney
   World® Auction, 1990
   (see Special Dolls)
   ....5,000.00
CHRISTMAS CANDY
   14" (36cm) *Classic
      Dolls*, 1993........100.00
CHRISTMAS CAROLING 10" (25cm) *Portrette Series*, 1992-1993 ....105.00
CHRISTMAS COOKIE 14" (36cm), 1992 ....115.00
CHRISTMAS EVE 14" (36cm) *Classic Dolls*, 1994 ....100.00
CHURCHILL, LADY 18" (46cm) hard plastic, *Beaux Arts Series*,
   1953 ....1,525.00
CHURCHILL, SIR WINSTON 18" (46cm) hard plastic, 1953..................1,235.00
CINDERELLA 7-8" (18-20cm) composition, 1935-1944 ....295.00
   9" (23cm) composition, 1936-1941...380.00
   16-18" (41-46cm) composition, 1935-1939 ....495.00 up
   14" (36cm) hard plastic, ball gown, 1950-1951...............................715.00
   14" (36cm) hard plastic, "poor" outfit, 1950-1951 ....660.00
   18" (46cm) hard plastic, 1950-1951 ....690.00
   8" (20cm) hard plastic, 1955 ....965.00
   12" (31cm) hard plastic, 1963 ....650.00 up
   14" (36cm) plastic/vinyl, "poor" outfit, 1967-1992 ....100.00

54

In 1953, the basic *Quiz-kins* 8in (20cm) all hard plastic dolls were available with yes and no buttons. They came in a painted hair version as well. *Marge Meisinger Collection. Photograph by Michael Cadotte.*

CINDERELLA *continued*

14" (36cm) plastic/vinyl, dressed in pink, 1970-1983........$ 92.00

blue ball gown, 1984-1986...........100.00

14" (36cm) Cinderella & trunk, made for Enchanted Doll House, 1985 *(see Special Dolls)* 375.00

14" (36cm) white ball gown, *Classic Dolls*, 1987-1991...............145.00

10" (25cm) Disney World®, 1989 *(see Special Dolls)*..700.00

10" (25cm) *Portrette Series*, 1990-1991.....75.00

8" (20cm) hard plastic, *Storyland Dolls*, 1990-1993.................55.00

8" (20cm) "poor" outfit, 1990-1991.................60.00

8" (20cm) "poor" outfit in blue w/black stripes, 1992..........................55.00

14" (36cm) white, gold ball gown, 1992......132.00

8" (20cm) blue ball gown, 1992-1994......65.00

CISSETTE Cissette introduced in 1957. 10" (25cm) tall, high heel feet. Jointed at the knee, hips, shoulder and neck. Prices for pristine dolls in original costumes, including undergarments and shoes. Allow more for mint-in-box dolls, those in rare costumes and those with fancy hairdos.

Beauty queen w/trophy, 1961 ....250.00
Coats and Hats 330.00
Formals..425.00
Pant outfits 270.00
Special gift set w/three wigs ....615.00 up
Street dresses...295.00

By 1953, the larger size all hard plastic dolls were the staple of the line. This is an 18in (46cm) *Winnie Walker* doll, featuring a Saran wig. *Marge Meisinger Collection. Photograph by Michael Cadotte.*

CISSY
20-21" (51-53cm) introduced with mature fashion body, jointed elbows, knees and high heel feet in 1955.

The Cissy face had been used previously on other dolls. Hundreds of outfits were produced for *Cissy*, not all appear in the catalog reprints. The *Cissy* doll body is subject to seam cracks on legs and necks, one should inspect the doll carefully before purchase. Many of the dolls have lost their cheek color. Prices are for mint dolls, with good face color in original costumes.

1955 white organdy gown trimmed in lace and red roses............$1,225.00
Ball gowns................790.00
Magazine ads, 1950s 24.00
Pant suits..310.00
Street dresses 365.00
Trunk/wardrobe..1,525.00
CISSY BRIDE 1921 21" (53cm) Companions, 8" (20cm) one-of-a-kind
Disneyland® 1993 *(see Special Dolls)*........................6,000.00
CISSY BY SCASSI 21" (53cm) made for FAO Schwarz, 1990
(see Special Dolls)..300.00
CLARA & THE NUTCRACKER 14" (36cm)........................90.00
CLARABELLE CLOWN 19" (48cm) 1951-1953........................392.00
29" (74cm) 625.00
49" (124cm) 800.00
CLAUDETTE 10" (25cm) *Portrette Series,* 1988-1989 ....72.00
CLAUS, MRS. 8" (20cm) mid-year release, 1993........................60.00
CLAUS, SANTA 8" (20cm) mid-year release, 1993........................70.00
CLEOPATRA 12" (31cm) *Portraits of History Series,* 1980-1985 ....52.00

This delightful *Peter Pan Quiz-kins*, is an 8in (20cm) all hard plastic doll from 1953 featuring buttons on his back to shake his head yes or no, that he doesn't want to grow up! *Marge Meisinger Collection. Photograph by Michael Cadotte.*

CLEVELAND, FRANCES
   1985-1987, 4th set,
   First Ladies Series...$ 85.00
CLOVER KID
   7" (18cm) composition,
   1935-1936.................345.00
CLOWN 8" (20cm)
      painted face, *Americana Series*, 1990-1992.....50.00
   Bobo 8" (20cm) hard
      plastic, 1991-1992....50.00
   Stilts 8" (20cm)
      1992-1993...............60.00
   Bubbles 8" (20cm)
      1993-1994................50.00
COCO 21" (53cm)
plastic/vinyl, in clothes other
than *Portrait*, 1966 ....1,825.00 up
   10" (25cm) *Portrette Series*, 1989-1992...............................69.00
COLLEEN 10" (25cm) *Portrette Series*, 1988 ....72.00
COLONIAL 7" (18cm) composition, 1937-1938................................280.00
   9" (23cm) composition, 1936-1939 ....292.00
COLONIAL GIRL 8" (20cm) hard plastic, bend knee walker, 1962-1964..375.00
COLUMBIAN SAILOR 12" (31cm) UFDC Luncheon, 1993
   (see Special Dolls)..350.00
COLUMBUS, CHRISTOPHER 8" (20cm) 1992 ....95.00
CONFEDERATE OFFICER 12" (31cm) *Scarlett Series*, 1991-1992 ....80.00
   8" (20cm) hard plastic, *Scarlett Series*, 1992 (Ashley) 55.00
COOKIE 19" (48cm) composition/cloth, 1938-1940 ....525.00
COOLIDGE, GRACE 14" (36cm) 6th set, *First Ladies Series*,
   1989-1990..100.00
CORNELIA
   16" (41cm) cloth/felt, 1930s 735.00
   21" (53cm) dressed in pink w/full cape, *Portrait Series*, 1972.........428.00
   pink w/3/4-length jacket (green eyed), 1973 ....365.00
   blue w/black trim, 1974 ....338.00
   rose red w/black trim and hat, 1975...338.00
   pink w/black trim and hat, 1976 ....318.00
   blue w/full cape, 1978..290.00
COSSACK 8" (20cm) 1989-1991 ....65.00
COUNTRY CHRISTMAS 14" (36cm) *Classic Dolls*, 1991-1992 ....132.00
COUNTRY COUSIN 10" (25cm) cloth, 1940s......................................865.00
   16-1/2" (42cm) vinyl, 1958..422.00

Off to Never Never Land go this enchanting set of all hard plastic *Peter Pan* and *Wendy*. They are 15in (38cm) tall and were made in 1953 only. *Marge Meisinger Collection. Photograph by Michael Cadotte.*

COURTNEY AND FRIENDS 8" (20cm) hard plastic, Alexander & 26" (66cm) porcelain, Günzel, 1992 *(see Special Dolls)*...........................$ 875.00

COUSIN GRACE 8" (20cm) hard plastic, bend knee walker, 1957 ....1,220.00

COUSIN KAREN 8" (20cm) hard plastic, bend knee walker, 1956 ....1,220.00

COWARDLY LION 8" (20cm) *Wizard of Oz Series*, 1993-1994 ....55.00

COWBOY 8" (20cm) hard plastic, bend knee, *Americana Series*, 1967-1969 ....368.00

8" (20cm) MADC, 1987 *(see Special Dolls)*...500.00

The Story Princess from television fame, was made in several different sizes and mediums over a span of several years. This is a 15in (38cm) all hard plastic doll from 1954. She is a coveted doll among collectors. *Marge Meisinger Collection. Photograph by Michael Cadotte*

COWGIRL 8" (20cm) hard plastic, bend knee, *Americana & Storyland Dolls*, 1966-1970...$ 365.00
10" (25cm) *Portrette Series*, 1990-1991.................65.00
CRETE 8" (20cm) straight legs, 1987.....................56.00
CROCKETT, DAVY (BOY OR GIRL) 8" (20cm) hard plastic, 1955...........................680.00
CROTIA 8" (20cm) hard plastic, *International Series*, 1994..................50.00
CRY DOLLY
14-16" (36-41cm) vinyl, 1953 ....190.00
14" (36cm), 16" (41cm), 19" (48cm) swimsuit 135.00
16-19" (41-48cm) all vinyl, dress or rompers...................157.00
CUDDLY
10-1/2" (27cm) cloth, 1942-1944 ....340.00
17" (43cm) cloth, 1942-1944...395.00
CURLY LOCKS
8" (20cm) hard plastic, 1955 ....865.00 up
8" (20cm) straight legs, *Storyland Dolls*, 1987-1988...................78.00
CUTE LITTLE BABY 14" (36cm) cloth/vinyl, 1994
dressed in pink stripe dress......................................80.00
dressed doll w/Layette and basket.............................200.00
CYNTHIA 15" (38cm) hard plastic, black hard plastic, 1952 ....765.00 up
18" (46cm) 1952 ....980.00 up
23" (58cm) 1952...1,225.00 up
CYRANO 8" (20cm) hard plastic, *Storyland Dolls*, 1994 ....60.00
CZECHOSLOVAKIA 7" (18cm) composition, 1935-1937 ....262.00
8" (20cm) hard plastic, bend knee, 1972..........................145.00
straight legs, 1973-1975 ....50.00
straight legs, 1976-1987 ....55.00
8" (20cm) white face, 1985-1987.................................55.00
8" (20cm) re-introduced 1992-1993 ....55.00

On every collector's want list is this fabulous 8in (20cm) all hard plastic Guardian Angel. She is a straight leg walker from 1954. The doll was also available as a strung doll in 1953. *Marge Meisinger Collection. Photograph by Michael Cadotte.*

DAFFY DOWN DILLEY 8" (20cm) straight legs, *Storyland Dolls*,
1986-1988 ....$ 72.00
8" (20cm) *Storyland Dolls*, 1987-1989 ....65.00
DAISY 10" (25cm), *Portrette Series*, 1987-1989 ....75.00
DANISH 7" (18cm) composition, 1937-1941 ....340.00
9" (23cm) composition, 1938-1940 ....365.00
DARE, VIRGINIA 9" (23cm) composition, 1940-1941 ....360.00
DARLENE
18" (46cm) cloth/vinyl, 1991-1992 ....105.00
DARLING, MRS.
10" (25cm) #1165, *Portrettes*, 1993-1994 ....100.00
DAVID & DIANA
8" (20cm) made for FAO Schwarz, 1989 *(see Special Dolls)*...............215.00
DAVID COPPERFIELD
16" (41cm) cloth, Dicken's character, early 1930s...................835.00
7" (18cm) composition, 1936-1938 ....362.00
14" (36cm) composition, 1938 ....765.00
DAVID QUACK-A-FIELD OR TWISTAIL cloth/felt, 1930s...............760.00
DAVID, THE LITTLE RABBI 8" (20cm) made for Celia's Dolls, 1991
(see Special Dolls) 92.00

Alice in Wonderland and *Through the Looking Glass* books by Lewis Carroll inspired many Alexander dolls. This very rare *Alice* is a straight leg walker 8in (20cm) and all hard plastic she dates from 1954. *Marge Meisinger Collection. Photograph by Michael Cadotte.*

DAY OF WEEK DOLLS
7" (18cm) composition,
1935-19.............$ 342.00
9-11" (23-28cm)
composition,
1936-1938..............365.00
13" (33cm)
composition,
1939.......................465.00
DEAREST
12" (31cm) vinyl baby,
1962-1964..............132.00
DECEMBER
14" (36cm) *Classic Dolls*, 1989.............102.00
DEFOE, DR.
14" (36cm) composition,
1937-1939...........1,422.00
DEGAS
21" (53cm) composition,
Portrait,   1945-1946 ....1,925.00 up
14" (36cm) "Dance Lesson" hard plastic/vinyl, *Classic Dolls*, 1994 ...75.00
DEGAS GIRL   14" (36cm) plastic/vinyl, *Portrait Children & Fine Art Series*, 1967-1987..95.00
DENMARK   10" (25cm) hard plastic, 1962-1963 ....718.00
8" (20cm) hard plastic, bend knee, 1970-1972............................155.00
8" (20cm) hard plastic, straight legs, 1973-1975 ....72.00
8" (20cm) hard plastic, straight legs, 1976-1989
(1985-1987 white face)..70.00
8" (20cm) re-introduced 1991 only 55.00
DIAMOND LIL
10" (25cm) MADC, 1993 *(see Special Dolls)*................................300.00
DIANA'S SUNDAY SOCIAL
8" (20cm) *Anne of Green Gables Series*, 1994.............................60.00
14" (36cm) *Anne of Green Gables Series*, 1994 ....100.00
DIANA'S TEA DRESS
14" (36cm) *Anne of Green Gables Series*, 1993 (doll and tea set) 115.00
DIANA'S TRUNK SET
Anne of Green Gables Series, 1993 (doll and wardrobe)..................250.00
Anne of Green Gables Series, 1994 (doll and wardrobe) costume change....250.00
14" (36cm) Winter coat..50.00
14" (36cm) School outfit, 1994 ....50.00
DICKENSON, EMILY   14" (36cm) *Classic Dolls*, 1989................98.00
DICKSIE & DUCKSIE   cloth/felt, 1930s.................................625.00

The Technicolor Rank production of *Romeo and Juliet* in 1954, inspired Madame Alexander to create this licensed set of 8in (20cm) hard plastic dolls for the 1955 line. *Marge Meisinger Collection. Photograph by Michael Cadotte.*

DILLY DALLY SALLY   7" (18cm) composition, 1937-1942.............$ 342.00
  9" (23cm) composition, 1938-1939 ....360.00
DING DONG DELL   7" (18cm) composition, 1937-1942.....................335.00
DINNER AT EIGHT   10" (25cm) *Portrette Series*, 1989-1991 ....60.00
DINOSAUR   8" (20cm) *Americana Series*, 1993-1994 ....50.00
DIONNE QUINTS   Original mint or very slight craze.
  8" (20cm) composition toddlers, molded hair and painted eyes,
    1935-1939..190.00 each, 1,225.00 set
  8" (20cm) composition toddlers, wigs and painted eyes,
    1938-1939..190.00 each, 1,225.00 set
  11" (28cm) composition toddlers, wigs and sleep eyes,
    1935-1938..370.00 each, 2,045.00 set
  11" (28cm) composition toddlers, molded hair and sleep eyes,
    1937-1938..370.00 each, 2,050.00 set
  11" (28cm) composition babies, wigs and sleep eyes,
    1936..325.00 each, 2,040.00 set
  11" (28cm) composition babies, molded hair and sleep eyes,
    1936..325.00 each, 2,045.00 set
  14" (36cm) composition toddlers, 1937-1938..........450.00 each, 2,500.00 set
  14" (36cm) cloth body, composition, 1938 ....525.00 each, 3,265.00 set
  16" (41cm) all cloth, 1935-1936......................................865.00 each
  16-17" (41-43cm) composition toddlers, 1937-1939..645.00 each, 3,625.00 set
  17" (43cm) cloth body, composition, 1938 ....565.00 each, 3,525.00 set

Davy Crockett is still as popular today as ever. He is an 8in (20cm) all hard plastic doll from 1955. Marge Meisinger Collection. Photograph by Michael Cadotte.

DIONNE QUINTS *continued*
19" (48cm) composition toddlers, 1936-1938 .$725.00 each, 4,235.00 set
20" (51cm) composition toddlers, 1938-1939 ....725.00 each, 4,235.00 set
22" (56cm) cloth/composition, 1936-1937...700.00 each
24" (61cm) all cloth, 1935-1936...$1,220.00 each

DOLLS OF THE MONTH
7-8" (18-20cm) composition, 1936-1938.....256.00 each

DOLLY 8" (20cm) *Storyland Dolls*, 1988-1989..........57.00

DOLLY LEVI
10" (25cm) *Portrette* (Matchmaker), 1994.....85.00

DOMINICAN REPUBLIC
8" (20cm) straight legs, 1986-1988 (1985-1986 white face)..............59.00

DOROTHY 8" (20cm) hard plastic, Storyland, *Wizard of Oz Series*, 1991-1994.................50.00
8" (20cm) hard plastic (*Emerald City*), mid-year release,1994......52.00
14" (36cm) all blue, white check dress, 1990-1993 ....84.00

DOTTIE DUMBUNNIE cloth/felt, 1930s 835.00
DRESSED FOR THE OPERA 18" (46cm) hard plastic, 1953................1,528.00
DRUCILLA 14" (36cm) MADC, 1992 *(see Special Dolls)* 200.00
DRUM MAJORETTE 7-1/2" (19cm) hard plastic, 1955 ....925.00
DUDE RANCH 8" (20cm) hard plastic, 1955 ....720.00
DUMPLIN' BABY 20 - 23-1/2" (51-60cm) 1957-1958 ....256.00
DUTCH 7" (18cm) composition, 1935-1939................332.00
9" (23cm) composition boy or girl, 1936-1941................365.00
8" (20cm) hard plastic boy*, bend knee walker, 1964................160.00
bend knee, 1965-1972 ....70.00-140.00
8" (20cm) hard plastic, straight legs, 1972-1973 ....58.00
8" (20cm) hard plastic girl*, bend knee walker, 1961-1964 ....167.00
8" (20cm) hard plastic, bend knee, 1965-1972 ....70.00-135.00
8" (20cm) bend knee walker, smile face, 1964 ....188.00

*Both became Netherland in 1974.

Ready for duty is the 8in (20cm) all hard plastic *Parlour Maid* from 1956. She is missing her feather duster, but is still a rare doll. *Marge Meisinger Collection. Photograph by Michael Cadotte.*

EASTER BONNET
14" (36cm)
1992 ....$ 145.00
EASTER BUNNY
8" (20cm) made for
A Child At Heart,
1991 *(see Special
Dolls)* ....265.00 up
EASTER DOLL
8" (20cm) hard plastic,
1968 ....1,225.00
14" (36cm) plastic/vinyl,
1968 ....765.00
EASTER SUNDAY
8" (20cm) black or
white, *Americana Series*,
1993 ....60.00
ECUADOR
8" (20cm) hard plastic,
bend knee and bend
knee walker,
1963-1966 ....370.00
EDITH, THE LONELY DOLL
8" (20cm) hard plastic,
1958 ....518.00
16" (41cm) plastic/vinyl,
1958-1959........256.00
22" (56cm)
1958-1959........345.00
EDITH WITH GOLDEN HAIR   18" (46cm) cloth, 1940s...........................625.00
EDWARDIAN   "so-called" 8" (20cm) hard plastic, 1953 ....975.00
"so-called" 18" (46cm) hard plastic, *Glamour Girl Series*, 1953....1,225.00
EISENHOWER, MAMIE   14" (36cm) 6th set, *First Ladies Series*,
1989-1990..100.00
EGYPT   8" (20cm) straight legs, 1986-1989 ....55.00
EGYPTIAN   7-8" (18-20cm) composition, 1936-1940........................340.00
9" (23cm) composition, 1936-1940 ....365.00
ELAINE 8" (20cm) hard plastic, matches 18" (46cm) 1954 ....1,225.00
18" (46cm) hard plastic, blue organdy dress, *Me and
My Shadow Series*, 1954..1,520.00

Shown in the 1956 catalog, this fantastic 8in (20cm) all hard plastic *Wendy* is dressed in a warm velvet costume. This red version is very rare, as most are dressed in green velvet. *Marge Meisinger Collection. Photograph by Michael Cadotte.*

ELISE 16-1/2" (42cm) hard plastic/vinyl arms, jointed ankles and knees, 1957-1964.
    Ballerina.............$ 365.00
    In ball gown...........622.00
    In street clothes......325.00
    Vinyl head, 1962....340.00
14" (36cm) plastic/vinyl, 1988......................92.00
17" (43cm) hard plastic/ vinyl one-piece arms and legs, jointed ankles and knees, 1961-1962...............225.00
17" (43cm) hard plastic/ vinyl, street dress 1966.......................220.00
17" (43cm) in trunk, trousseau, 1966-1972...............762.00
17" (43cm) *Portrait*, 1972-1973...............190.00
17" (43cm) in formal, 1966, 1976-197 ....185.00
17" (43cm) Bride, 1966-1987 ....192.00
17"(43cm) Ballerina, 1966-1991...90.00
17" (43cm) Elise in discontinued costumes, 1966-1989 ....162.00 up
18" (46cm) w/bouffant hairstyle, 1963 ....328.00
18" (46cm) hard plastic/vinyl, jointed ankles and knees, 1963-1964 ....225.00
    In riding habit...362.00
ELIZA 14" (36cm) *Classic Dolls*, 1991 ....155.00
EMILY cloth/felt, 1930s...725.00
EMPEROR & NIGHTINGALE one-of-a-kind 1992 Disney World® Auction *(see Special Dolls)*...5,200.00
EMPRESS ELISABETH 10" (25cm) made for My Doll House, 1991 *(see Special Dolls)* 140.00

Little Women dolls are very popular with collectors. These 12in (31cm) hard plastic dolls were manufactured from 1957 until the mid-1960s. *Laurie*, with a hard plastic head, is from 1966 only and is very hard to find. *Marge Meisinger Collection. Photograph by Michael Cadotte.*

ENCHANTED DOLL   *(see Special Dolls)*
   8" (20cm) rick-rack pinafore, lace trim, 1980 ....$ 322.00
   8" (20cm) eyelet pinafore, eyelet trim, 1981 ....300.00
   10" (25cm) hard plastic, 1988 *(see Special Dolls)* ....175.00 up
ENCHANTED EVENING
   21" (53cm) Portrait, 1991 (uses vinyl *Cissy* mold)............................200.00
ENGLISH GUARD
   8" (20cm) hard plastic, bend knee, 1966-1968 ....269.00
   8" (20cm) re-introduced 1989-1991...55.00
ESKIMO
   9" (23cm) composition, 1936-1939..282.00
   8" (20cm) hard plastic, bend knee, *Americana Series*, 1966-1969....365.00
   W/smile face..422.00
ESTONIA   8" (20cm) straight legs, 1986-1987 ....89.00
EVA LOVELACE   7" (18cm) composition, 1935................................337.00
   Cloth, 1935 ....625.00
EVANGELINE   18" (46cm) cloth, 1930s ....718.00 up

The Royal Family was once again the subject of this 10in (25cm) all hard plastic *Cissette Queen*, dressed in gold brocade and made in 1957. *Marge Meisinger Collection. Photograph by Michael Cadotte.*

FAIRY GODMOTHER Outfit, MADC, 1983 (not an Alexander outfit).$ 400.00
14" (36cm) *Classic Dolls*, 1983-1992....75.00-165.00
10" (25cm) *Portrettes*, 1993.........................85.00

FAIRY PRINCESS
7-8" (18-20cm) composition, 1940-1943....295.00
9" (23cm) composition, 1939-1941..............322.00
11" (28cm) composition, 1939-1943..............365.00
15-18" (38-46cm) composition, 1939-1943....620.00
21-22" (53-56cm) composition, 1939-1946..............968.00

FAIRY QUEEN
14-1/2" (37cm) composition, 1940-1946....620.00
18" (46cm) composition, 1940-1946..............768.00
14-1/2" (37cm) hard plastic, 1948-1950..685.00
18" (46cm) hard plastic, 1949-1950..............902.00

FAIRY TALES - DUMAS
9" (23cm) composition, 1937-1941...322.00

FAITH 8" (20cm) hard plastic, *Americana Series*, 1961..................1,215.00 up
8" (20cm) hard plastic, CU Gathering, 1992 *(see Special Dolls)* 225.00

FANNIE ELIZABETH 8" (20cm) made for Belk & Leggett, 1991 *(see Special Dolls)*...70.00

FARMER'S DAUGHTER 8" (20cm) made for Enchanted Doll House, 1991 *(see Special Dolls)*...125.00

FARMER'S DAUGHTER Goes To Town cape and basket added, made for Enchanted Doll House, 1992 *(see Special Dolls)* 90.00

FASHIONS OF THE CENTURY 14-18" (36-46cm) hard plastic, 1954-1955 ....1,525.00

FATHER CHRISTMAS 8" (20cm) hard plastic, *Americana Series*, 1994.....65.00

FILLMORE, ABIGAIL 3rd set, *First Ladies Series*, 1982-1984 ....90.00

FINDLAY, JANE 1st set, *First Ladies Series*, 1979-1981 ....118.00

FINLAND 8" (20cm) hard plastic, bend knee, 1968-1972 ....132.00
8" (20cm) hard plastic, straight legs, 1973-1975 ....72.00
8" (20cm) hard plastic, straight legs, 1976-1987 ....58.00

FINNISH 7" (18cm) composition, 1935-1937...................................267.00

The Lissy molds were used for this 12in (31cm) all hard plastic *Kelly*, made in 1959. This is a very popular doll with collectors. *Marge Meisinger Collection. Photograph by Michael Cadotte.*

FIRST COMMUNION
8" (20cm) hard plastic,
    1957................$ 665.00
14" (36cm) *Classic Dolls*,
    1991-1992.............95.00
8" (20cm) hard plastic,
Americana Series,
    1994......................60.00

First Ladies
1st set, 1976-1978 ....800.00
2nd set, 1979-1981 ....650.00
3rd set, 1982-1984 ....650.00
4th set, 1985-1987 ....650.00
5th set, 1988 ....650.00
6th set, 1989-1990 ....600.00

FISHER QUINTS
"so-called" 7" (18cm) hard
    plastic/vinyl,
    1964 set 450.00

FIVE LITTLE PEPPERS
13" (33cm) & 16" (41cm)
    composition,
    1936.........................665.00 each

FLAPPER 10" (25cm) *Portrette Series*, 1988-1991...............................47.00
10" (25cm) MADC, 1988 *(see Special Dolls)*....................................250.00
FLORA MCFLIMSEY 9" (23cm) composition, 1938-1941....................345.00
14" (36cm) composition, 1938-1944..475.00
15-16" (38-41cm) composition, 1938-1944 ....550.00
16-17" (41-43cm) composition, 1936-1937 ....565.00
22" (56cm) composition, 1938-1944...750.00
15" (38cm) *Miss Flora McFlimsey*, vinyl head, 1953 ....620.00
FLOWER GIRL 16-18" (41-46cm) composition, 1939, 1944-1947 ......585.00
20-24" (51-61cm) composition, 1939, 1944-1947 ....800.00
15" (38cm) hard plastic, 1954 ....635.00
15-18" (38-46cm) hard plastic, 1954..445.00
8" (20cm) hard plastic, 1956 ....675.00
10" (25cm) *Portrette Series*, 1988-1990 ....78.00
8" (20cm) hard plastic, black or white doll, *Americana Series*, 1992.....55.00
FRANCE 7" (18cm) composition, 1936-1943 ....290.00
8" (20cm) hard plastic, *International Series*, 1994 ....50.00

68

A 14in (36cm) *Shari Lewis* from 1959. This doll and her 21in (53cm) companion, featured an exclusive mold designed just for this doll. This practice is very uncommon to Alexander dolls, as most characters are created from existing molds. *A. Glenn Mandeville Collection.*

FRENCH
  9" (23cm) composition,
    1937-1941.........................$ 290.00
  8" (20cm) hard plastic,
    bend knee walker,
    1961-1965............................185.00
  8" (20cm) hard plastic,
    bend knee,
    1965-1972............................155.00
  8" (20cm) hard plastic,
    straight legs,
    1973-1975.............................82.00
  white face, 1985.......................75.00
  8" (20cm) straight legs, 1976-1992 ....52.00
FRENCH ARISTOCRAT 10" (25cm) *Portrette*, 1991 ....105.00
FRENCH FLOWER GIRL 8" (20cm) hard plastic, 1956 ....675.00
FRIAR TUCK 8" (20cm) hard plastic, 1989-1990 ....45.00
FRIEDRICH *(see Sound of Music)*
FROG PRINCE AND PRINCESS 8" (20cm) doll and a Steiff bear,
  one-of-a-kind, Disney World® Auction *(see Special Dolls)* 5,300.00
FROU-FROU 40" (101cm) all cloth, yarn hair, ballerina in green,
  lilac, 1951 only 738.00
FUNNY 18" (46cm) cloth, 1963-1977...72.00
FUNNY MAGGIE 8" (20cm) hard plastic, *Storyland Dolls*, 1994 ....50.00

Helen Pessell cosmetics was the inspiration for this 8in (20cm) hard plastic doll offered in 1960 only. Most dolls had the smile face and lighter hair, rather than the face shown here. She came in a gift box with toiletries. *Marge Meisinger Collection. Photograph by Michael Cadotte.*

GAINSBOROUGH
10" (25cm) pink, full dress, hat, 1957........$ 470.00
20" (51cm) hard plastic, taffeta gown, picture hat, *Models Formals Series*, 1957......1,100.00
21" (53cm) hard plastic/ vinyl arms, blue w/white lace jacket, 1968......................700.00
21" (53cm) bright blue w/full ecru overlace, 1972....................570.00
21" (53cm) pale blue, scallop lace overskirt, 1973....................500.00
21" (53cm) pink w/full lace overdress, 1978....................370.00

GARDEN PARTY
18" (46cm) hard plastic, 1953 ....1,265.00
8" (20cm) hard plastic, 1955 ....855.00
20" (51cm) hard plastic, 1956-1957 ....925.00

GARFIELD, LUCRETIA
4th set, *First Ladies Series*, 1985-1987............................120.00

GENIUS BABY 21-30" (53-76cm) plastic/vinyl, flirty eyes, 1960-1961.....180.00
Little, 8" (20cm) hard plastic head/vinyl, 1956-1962 (*see Little Genius*)

GEPPETTO 8" (20cm) *Storyland Dolls*, 1993-1994 ....45.00

GERANIUM 9" (23cm) early vinyl toddler, red organdy dress and bonnet, 1953..135.00

GERMAN (GERMANY) 8" (20cm) hard plastic, bend knee, 1966-1972 ....150.00
8" (20cm) hard plastic, straight legs, 1973-1975....................80.00
8" (20cm) white face, 1986..70.00
8" (20cm) straight legs, 1976-1991 ....55.00
8" (20cm) hard plastic, *International Series*, 1994..................50.00

GIBSON GIRL 16" (41cm) cloth, 1930s............................825.00
10" (25cm) hard plastic, eye shadow, 1962...........................650.00
plain blouse w/no stripes, 1963 ....650.00 up
10" (25cm) *Portrette Series*, 1988-1990.............................60.00

GIDGET 14" (36cm) plastic/vinyl, 1966...........................355.00

GIGI 14" (36cm) *Classic Dolls*, 1986-1987.......................90.00

GILBERT 8" (20cm) hard plastic, *Anne of Green Gables Series*, 1994....$ 50.00
GLAMOUR GIRLS 18" (46cm) hard plastic, 1953................................1,300.00
GLINDA, THE GOOD WITCH 8" (20cm) *Wizard of Oz Series*, 1992-1994 .....60.00
   14" (36cm) *Wizard of Oz Series*, 1994 ....100.00
GODEY 21" (53cm) composition, 1945-1947................................1,300.00
   20" (51cm) hard plastic, 1951..1,575.00
   14" (36cm) hard plastic, 1950-1951 ....1,265.00
   18" (46cm) hard plastic, *Glamour Girls Series*, 1953 ....1,365.00
   8" (20cm) straight leg walker, 1955...1,255.00
   21" (53cm) hard plastic/vinyl straight arms, red faille gown,
     matching coat, black braid trim coat has black marabou's collar,
     straw hat, 1960...975.00
   21" (53cm) hard plastic/vinyl straight arms, lavender purple
     hat and coat, 1961..1,280.00
   21" (53cm) dressed in all red, blonde hair, 1965............................700.00
   21" (53cm) plastic/vinyl, red w/black short jacket and hat, 1966............2,075.00
   21" (53cm) hard plastic/vinyl arms, dressed in pink & ecru, 1967.........625.00
   10" (25cm) hard plastic, dressed in all pink w/bows down front, 1968......500.00
   10" (25cm) all yellow w/bows down front, 1969.............................500.00
   21" (53cm) red w/black trim, 1969..525.00
   10" (25cm) all lace pink dress w/natural straw hat, 1970.................525.00
   21" (53cm) pink w/burgundy short jacket, 1970 ....365.00
   21" (53cm) pink, black trim, short jacket, 1971 ....375.00
   21" (53cm) ecru w/red jacket and bonnet, 1977...........................355.00
GODEY BRIDE 14" (36cm) hard plastic, 1950...............................900.00
   18" (46cm) hard plastic, 1950-1951 ....1,000.00
GODEY GROOM 14" (36cm) hard plastic, 1950 ....950.00
   18" (46cm) hard plastic, 1950-1951 ....1,565.00
GODEY LADY 14" (36cm) hard plastic, 1950 ....1,000.00
   18" (46cm) hard plastic, 1950-1951 ....1,545.00
GOLD RUSH 10" (25cm) hard plastic, 1963 ....1,525.00
GOLDFISH 8" (20cm) *Americana Series*, 1993-1994 ....70.00
GOLDILOCKS 18" (46cm) cloth, 1930s..800.00
   7-8" (18-20cm) composition, 1938-1942.....................................325.00
   14" (36cm) plastic/vinyl, satin dress, *Classic Dolls*, 1978-1979.........120.00
   14" (36cm) cotton dress, 1980-1983 ....110.00
   8" (20cm) *Storyland Dolls*, 1990-1991 (1991 dress is different plaid)........55.00
   14" (36cm) long side curls, *Classic Dolls*, 1991 ....95.00
   8" (20cm) hard plastic, *Storyland Dolls*, 1994 ....60.00
GONE WITH THE WIND 14" (36cm) all white dress/green sash, 1968-1986..125.00 up
GOOD FAIRY 14" (36cm) hard plastic, 1947-1949 ....700.00
GOOD LITTLE GIRL 16" (41cm) cloth, wears pink dress, mate to
  Bad Little Girl, 1966 ....135.00
GOYA 8" (20cm) hard plastic, 1953 ....1,000.00
   21" (53cm) hard plastic/vinyl arms, multi-tier pink dress, 1968.........600.00
   21" (53cm) maroon dress w/black Spanish lace, 1982-1983 ....275.00
GRADUATION 8" (20cm) hard plastic, 1957................................875.00
   12" (31cm) hard plastic, 1957...895.00
   8" (20cm) white doll, *Americana Series*, 1990-1992 ....55.00

Every collector would love this charming 8in (20cm) all hard plastic *Maggie Mix-up* from 1960. She is mint in her box, with original wrist booklet. *Marge Meisinger Collection. Photograph by Michael Cadotte.*

GRADUATION *continued*
8" (20cm) white or black doll, 1991-1992 $ 55.00
GRANDMA JANE
14" (36cm) plastic/vinyl, 1970-1972......245.00
GRANT, JULIA
3rd set, *First Ladies Series*, 1982-1984........98.00
GRAVE, ALICE
18" (46cm)
cloth, 1930s 700.00
GREAT BRITAIN 8" (20cm) hard plastic, 1977-1988....................62.00
GREECE 8" (20cm) *International Dolls*, 1993 ....47.00
GREECE (BOY) 8" (20cm) hard plastic, 1992-1993....................52.00
GREEK BOY 8" (20cm) hard plastic, bend knee walker, 1965 ....455.00
bend knee, 1966-1968....................375.00
GREEK GIRL 8" (20cm) hard plastic, bend knee, 1968-1972 ....125.00
8" (20cm) hard plastic, straight legs, 1973-1975....................75.00
8" (20cm) hard plastic, straight legs, 1976-1987....................70.00
GRETEL 7" composition, 1935-1942....................310.00
9" (23cm) composition, 1938-1940 ....340.00
7-1/2–8" (19-20cm) hard plastic, straight leg walker, 1955................555.00
18" (46cm) hard plastic, 1948....................995.00 up
8" (20cm) hard plastic, bend knee, *Storyland Dolls*, 1966-1972 ....155.00
8" (20cm) hard plastic, straight legs, 1973-1975....................75.00
8" (20cm) hard plastic, straight legs, 1976-1986....................75.00
8" (20cm) hard plastic, *Storyland Dolls*, re-introduced, 1991-1992........50.00
GRETL *(see Sound of Music)*
GROOM 18-21" (46-53cm) composition, 1946-1947 ....955.00
18-21" (46-53cm) hard plastic, 1949-1951....................820.00 up
7-1/2" (19cm) hard plastic, 1953-1955 ....465.00
14-16" (36-41cm) hard plastic, 1949-1951....................800.00 up
8" (20cm) hard plastic, 1956-1958, 1961-1963 ....370.00
8" (20cm) *Americana Series*, 1990....................60.00
8" (20cm) re-issue, 1993....................55.00
GUENIVERE 10" (25cm) *Portrette Series*, 1992....................95.00

H **HALLOWEEN**
8" (20cm) made for Greenville Show, 1990 *(see Special Dolls)*...$160.00
HAMLET 12" (31cm) *Romance Collection*....................100.00
12" (31cm) #1312, 1993 ....90.00

A personal favorite are the 17in (43cm) hard plastic and vinyl *Maggie Mix-up* dolls. This freckle faced imp was manufactured in 1960-1961. This version is stock number 1811 and is only missing her heart necklace. *Marge Meisinger Collection. Photograph by Michael Cadotte.*

HANSEL
7" (18cm) composition,
   1935-1942..................$ 325.00
9" (23cm) composition,
   1938-1940......................340.00
18" (46cm) hard plastic,
   1948..............................725.00
8" (20cm) hard plastic, straight
   leg walker, 1955..............550.00
8" (20cm) hard plastic, bend
   knee, *Storyland Dolls*,
   1966-1972......................148.00
8" (20cm) hard plastic,
   straight legs,
   1973-1975........................75.00
8" (20cm) hard plastic, straight
   legs, 1976-1986................70.00
8" (20cm) hard plastic,
   Storyland Dolls, re-introduced
   1991-1992........................52.00

HAPPY 20" (51cm) cloth/
vinyl, 1970.....................225.00

HAPPY BIRTHDAY 8" (20cm) hard plastic, black or white doll,
Americana Series, 1992-1993..50.00
8" (20cm) hard plastic, white only, *Americana Series*,
   minor costume change, 1994 ....60.00
14" (36cm) *Classic Dolls*, 1994 ....90.00

HAPPY BIRTHDAY BILLY 8" (20cm) black or white,
Americana Series, 1993 ....55.00

HAPPY BIRTHDAY MADAME 8" (20cm) MADC, 1985
(see Special Dolls) 365.00

HARDING, FLORENCE 5th set, *First Ladies Series,* 1988 ....100.00

HARMONY 21" (53cm) porcelain, w/8" (20cm) hard plastic
Alexander nymph, one-of-a-kind by Hildegard Gunzel, Disney
World® Auction, 1992 *(see Special Dolls)* 7,500.00

HARMONY AND CHERUB 8" (20cm) doll and Hildegard Günzel
doll, one-of-a-kind Disney World® Auction, 1993
(see Special Dolls) 850.00

HARRISON, CAROLINE 4th set, *First Ladies Series,* 1985-1987.................100.00

HAWAII 8" (20cm) *Americana Series,* 1990-1991.....................................55.00

HAWAIIAN 7" (18cm) composition, 1936-1939 ....310.00
9" (23cm) composition, 1937-1944 ....360.00
8" (20cm) hard plastic, bend knee, *Americana Series*, 1966-1969............470.00

A 15in (38cm) *Caroline* from 1961, stands with a 1962 21in (53cm) *Jacqueline* doll. Both dolls are vinyl and hard plastic. The outfit on the 21in (53cm) *Jacqueline* was not featured in a catalog. The outfit is titled Embassy Tea, but that is unsubstantiated. *Marge Meisinger Collection. Photograph by Michael Cadotte.*

HAYES, LUCY
   4th set,
   First Ladies Series,
   1985-1987.......$ 102.00
HEATHER
   18" (46cm) cloth/vinyl,
   1990-1993............85.00
HEIDI
   7" (18cm) composition,
      1938-1939.......300.00
   14" (36cm) plastic/
      vinyl, *Classic Dolls,*
      1969-1988.......100.00
   8" (20cm) hard plastic, *Storyland Dolls,* 1991-1992 ....55.00
HELLO BABY 22" (56cm) 1962...185.00
HENIE, SONJA 7" (18cm) composition, 1939-1942 ....385.00
   9" (23cm) composition, 1940-1941 ....500.00
   11" (28cm) composition..600.00
   13-15" (33-38cm) composition, 1939-1942....................................650.00
   14" (36cm) composition..600.00-700.00
   14" (36cm) in case, wardrobe..1,200.00 up
   17-18" (43-46cm) composition 675.00-785.00
   20-23" (51-58cm) composition 775.00-900.00
   13-14" (33-36cm) composition, jointed waist 650.00-750.00
   15-18" (38-46cm) hard plastic/vinyl, no extra joints, 1951 only.......875.00
HIAWATHA 18" (46cm) cloth, early 1930s 720.00
   7" (18cm) composition 305.00
   8" (20cm) hard plastic, *Americana Series,* 1967-1969 ....372.00
HIGHLAND FLING 8" (20cm) hard plastic, 1955 ....550.00
HOLIDAY ON ICE 8" (20cm) hard plastic, 1992
   (some tagged *Christmas on Ice*)...55.00
HOLLAND 7" (18cm) composition, 1936-1943 ....268.00
HOLLY 10" (25cm) *Portrette Series,* 1990-1991 ....85.00
HOMECOMING 8" (20cm) hard plastic, MADC, 1993
   (see Special Dolls)...150.00
HONEYBEAR 12" (31cm) vinyl, 1963.....................................175.00 up
HONEYBUN 18-19" (46-48cm) cloth/vinyl, 1951-1952.......................195.00
   23-26" (58-66cm) 315.00
HONEYETTE BABY 7" (18cm) composition, little girl dress, 1934-1937..350.00
   16" (41cm) composition/cloth, 1941-1942................................215.00
HOOVER, LOU 14" (36cm) plastic, 6th set, *First Ladies Series,*
   1989-1990...100.00

The impish *Maggie Mix-up* in 1961 was dressed as an angel. She is an 8in (20cm) hard plastic doll. The outfit was also sold separately. *Marge Meisinger Collection. Photograph by Michael Cadotte.*

HOPE 8" (20cm)
CU Gathering, 1993
(see Special Dolls)...$ 250.00
HUCKLEBERRY FINN
8" (20cm) hard plastic,
Storyland Dolls,
1989-1991.................60.00
HUGGUMS, BIG
25" (64cm) Lively,
knob moves head and
limbs, 1963............125.00
25" (64cm) boy or
girl, 1963-1979......125.00
HUGGUMS, LITTLE
12" (31cm) rooted hair,
1963-1982, 1988......55.00
12" (31cm) molded hair,
1963-1992................55.00
14" (36cm) molded hair,
1986.........................50.00
12" (31cm) special outfits
for Imaginarium Shop,
1991................50.00-55.00

HULDA 18" (46cm) hard plastic, 1947 ....1,600.00 up
HUNGARIAN (HUNGARY) 8" (20cm) hard plastic, bend knee walker,
1962-1965 ....198.00
bend knee or bend knee walker with metal crown 175.00
bend knee, 1965-1972...155.00
8" (20cm) hard plastic, straight legs, 1973-1976.............................75.00
8" (20cm) hard plastic, straight legs, 1976-1986.............................70.00
8" (20cm) hard plastic, re-introduced 1992-1993............................50.00

This 10in (25cm) *Margot* from 1961, illustrates the heavy cats eye make-up and upswept hair styles that were popular during the period. This formal is a desirable version of this all hard plastic doll. *Marge Meisinger Collection. Photograph by Michael Cadotte.*

IBIZA
  8" (20cm) 1989 .....$ 115.00
ICE SKATER 8" (20cm)
  bend knee and bend
  knee walker,
  1955-1956 ....625.00
  8" (20cm) *Americana
  Series*, 1990-1991 .....60.00
ICELAND 10" (25cm)
  1962-1963 ....750.00 up
INDIA 8" (20cm) hard
  plastic, bend knee
  walker, 1965 ....265.00
  8" (20cm) hard plastic,
  bend knee,
  1965-1972 ....170.00
  8" (20cm) hard plastic,
  bend knee and bend
  knee walker, white ..170.00
  8" (20cm) hard plastic, straight legs, 1973-1975 ....95.00
  8" (20cm) hard plastic, straight legs, 1976-1988 ....85.00
INDIAN BOY 8" (20cm) hard plastic, bend knee, *Americana Series*, 1966.....400.00
INDIAN GIRL 8" (20cm) hard plastic, bend knee, *Americana Series*, 1966.....425.00
INDONESIA 8" (20cm) hard plastic, bend knee, 1970-1972 ....180.00
  Smile face, bend knee, 1970s (some years)......................248.00
  8" (20cm) hard plastic, straight legs, 1972-1975 ....88.00
  8" (20cm) hard plastic, straight legs, 1976-1988 ....80.00
INGALLS, LAURA 14" (36cm) *Classic Dolls*, 1989-1991 ....85.00
INGRES 14" (36cm) plastic/vinyl, *Fine Arts Series*, 1987 ....110.00
IRIS 10" (25cm) hard plastic, 1987-1988 ....110.00
IRISH (IRELAND) 8" (20cm) hard plastic, bend knee walker, 1965 ......215.00
  8" (20cm) bend knee, gown, 1966-1972...............................165.00
  8" (20cm) straight legs, gown, 1973-1975.............................75.00
  8" (20cm) straight legs, 1976-1985.......................................70.00
  8" (20cm) straight legs, 1985-1987.......................................65.00
  8" (20cm) straight legs, short dress, 1987-1992 ....50.00
ISOLDE 14" (36cm) *Opera Series*, 1985-1986.......................110.00
ISRAEL 8" (20cm) hard plastic, bend knee, 1965-1972.......................140.00
  8" (20cm) hard plastic, straight legs, 1973-1975 ....70.00
  8" (20cm) hard plastic, straight legs, 1976-1988 ....65.00
ITALIAN 8" (20cm) hard plastic, bend knee walker, 1962-1964 ....172.00
  8" (20cm) hard plastic, bend knee, 1965-1972................................150.00
  8" (20cm) hard plastic, straight legs, 1973................................72.00

One of the great larger sized dolls from the Alexander Doll Company is this *Mimi* with a vinyl head and multi-jointed body. She is 30in (76cm) tall and is from 1961. *Marge Meisinger Collection. Photograph by Michael Cadotte.*

ITALY   8" (20cm) hard plastic, straight legs,
1974-1984..................$ 72.00
White face, 1985...............68.00
8" (20cm) hard plastic, straight legs, 1986-1991...65.00
8" (20cm) hard plastic, straight legs, 1992-1994..55.00

IT'S A GIRL   21" (53cm) hard plastic/vinyl and 8" (20cm) hard plastic baby, one-of-a-kind, Disney World® Auction, 1992 *(see Special Dolls)*...........................13,500.00

Katie is a 12in (31cm) all hard plastic doll made for the 100th anniversary of FAO Schwarz in 1962. Her companion was *Tommy*, made from the same molds. A wooden rocking horse came with the dolls. *Marge Meisinger Collection. Photograph by Michael Cadotte.*

JACK AND JILL
7" (18cm) composition,
1938-1943 ......$ 315.00 each
9" (23cm) composition,
1939....................330.00 each
8" (20cm) straight legs, *Storyland Dolls*,
1987-1992 ....68.00 each
JACK BE NIMBLE
8" (20cm) hard plastic, made for Dolly Dears, 1993
(see Special Dolls)..150.00
JACKSON, SARAH   2nd set, *First Ladies Series*,
1979-1981..............120.00
JACQUELINE   21" (53cm) hard plastic/vinyl arms, street dress, suit, 1961-1962............................700.00
Ball gown..855.00
In trunk w/wardrobe, 1962, 1966-1967 ....1,250.00 up
In riding habit, 1962 ....620.00
In gown from cover of 1962 catalog 750.00
10" (25cm) hard plastic, 1962...600.00
JAMAICA   8" (20cm) straight legs, 1986-1988 ....75.00
JANIE   12" (31cm) toddler, 1964-1966 ....320.00
Ballerina, 1965..295.00
14" (36cm) baby, 1972-1973 ....85.00
20" (51cm) baby, 1972-1973..110.00

Madame Alexander loved Jacqueline Kennedy and made several versions of a *Jacqueline* doll.This 10in (25cm) all hard plastic doll dates from 1962. *Marge Meisinger Collection. Photograph by Michael Cadotte.*

JAPAN 8" (20cm)
    hard plastic, bend knee,
    1968-1972.$ 130.00
  8" (20cm) hard
    plastic, straight legs,
    1973-1975 .....85.00
  8" (20cm) hard plastic,
    straight legs,
    1976-1986 ......70.00
  8" (20cm)
    1987-1990......72.00
  8" (20cm) hard plastic,
    white face,
    re-introduced
    1992-1993.....60.00
JASMINE 10" (25cm)
  Portrette Series,
  1987-1988 ....90.00

JEANNIE WALKER 13-14" (33-36cm) composition, 1940s 445.00
  18" (46cm) composition, 1940s 550.00
JENNIFER'S TRUNK SET 14" (36cm) doll and wardrobe, 1990..............245.00
JESSICA 18" (46cm) cloth/vinyl, 1990.......................................145.00
JO *(see Little Women)*
JOANIE 36" (91cm) plastic/vinyl, 1960-1961 ....500.00 up
  36" (91cm) Nurse, all white w/black band on cap, 1960...................400.00 up
  36" (91cm) Nurse, colored dress, all white pinafore and cap, 1961...425.00
JOHN 8" (20cm) *Storyland Dolls*, 1993...45.00
JOHN POWER'S MODELS 14" (36cm) hard plastic, 1952 (mint) ....1,550.00 up
  18" (46cm) hard plastic, 1952 (mint)...1,350.00 up
JONES, CASEY 8" (20cm) hard plastic, *Americana Series*, 1991-1992 ...52.00
JOSEPHINE 12" (31cm) *Portraits of History*, 1980-1986.......................70.00
  21" (53cm) hard plastic/vinyl, *Portrait Series*, 1994 ....300.00
JOY 12" (31cm) porcelain, New England Collectors, 1990
  (see Special Dolls)...270.00
JUDY 21" (53cm) hard plastic/vinyl arms, 1962 (catalog special) 1,745.00
JUGO-SLAV 7" (18cm) composition, 1935-1937...............................280.00
JULIET 18" (46cm) composition, 1937-40......................................1,255.00
  21" (53cm) composition, *Portrait Series*, 1945-1946......................1,950.00
  8" (20cm) hard plastic, 1955......................................845.00-950.00
  12" (31cm) plastic/vinyl, *Portrait Children Series*, 1978-1987...........60.00
  12" (31cm) *Romance Collection*, re-introduced 1991-1992 ....105.00
  8" (20cm) hard plastic, *Storyland Collection*, mid-year release, 1994 ....100.00
JUNE BRIDE 21" (53cm) composition, *Portrait Series*, 1939,
  1946-1947...1,750.00-1,950.00

An all hard plastic 8in (20cm) doll was made in 1962-1964 and called *Colonial Girl*. She was a bend knee walker and had the basket illustrated.This name would be changed to *Priscilla* in 1965 with a non-walking doll and a different basket. *Marge Meisinger Collection.* *Photograph by Michael Cadotte.*

JUNE WEDDING
  8" (20cm) hard plastic,
  1956...........................$ 725.00
KAREN BALLERINA
  15" (38cm) composition,
  1947-1949......................750.00
  18-21" (46-53cm)............825.00
  15-18" (38-46cm) hard
  plastic, 1948-1949........900.00
KATE GREENAWAY
  16" (41cm) cloth,
  1936-1938.....................925.00
  7" (18cm) composition,
  1938-1943.....................385.00
  9" (23cm) composition,
  1936-1939.....................390.00
  13" (33cm) composition,
  1938-1943.....................645.00
  18" (46cm) composition,
  1938-1943.....................750.00
  24" (61cm) composition,
  1938-1943.....................885.00
  14" (36cm) *Classic Dolls*,
  1993.............................120.00
KATHLEEN TODDLER
  23" (58cm) rigid vinyl, 1959...145.00
KATHY   15-18" (38-46cm) hard plastic, has braids,1949-1951 ....750.00-950.00
KATHY BABY   13-15" (33-38cm) vinyl, rooted or molded hair,
  1954-1956..80.00-135.00
  11" (28cm) vinyl, molded hair, w/trousseau, 1955-1956.......................140.00
  11-13" (28-33cm) vinyl, rooted or molded hair, 1955-1956 ....75.00-135.00
  18-21" (46-53cm) rooted or molded hair, 1954-1956 ....150.00-200.00
  21" (53cm) 1954 ....190.00
  21" (53cm) and 25" (64cm) 1955-1956...............................150.00-250.00
KATHY CRY DOLLY   11-15" (28-38cm) vinyl, 1957-1958 ....75.00-90.00
  18" (46cm), 21" (53cm), 25" (64cm) 95.00-150.00
KATHY TEARS   11" (28cm), 15" (38cm), 17" (43cm) vinyl,
  closed mouth, 1959-1962...70.00-100.00
  19" (48cm), 23" (58cm), 26" (66cm) 1959-1962 ....120.00-175.00
  12" (31cm), 16" (41cm), 19" (48cm) vinyl, 1960-1961..............80.00-100.00
KATIE (BLACK SMARTY)   12" (31cm) plastic/vinyl, 1963.......................385.00
KATIE   12" (31cm) hard plastic, made for FAO Schwarz 100th
  Anniversary, 1962 ....1,300.00
  12" (31cm) *Black Janie*, 1965..400.00
KEANE, DORIS   cloth, 1930s 850.00
  9-11" (23-28cm) composition, 1936-1937......................................310.00

Madame Alexander was famous for her award winning ballgowns. This version of *Elise* was offered around 1963 and features a 16in (41cm) doll with a hard plastic head. *Marge Meisinger Collection. Photograph by Michael Cadotte.*

KELLY 12" (31cm) hard plastic,
    1959 ....$ 455.00
    15-16" (38-41cm)
    1958-1959.......................350.00
    16" (41cm) in trunk, wardrobe,
    1959 ....515.00
    22" (56cm) 1958-1959 .....490.00
KENNEDY, JACQUELINE
    14" (36cm) 6th set, *First Ladies Series*, 1989-1990 ....185.00
KITTEN 24" (61cm) rooted hair,
1961...110.00
14-18" (36-46cm) cloth/vinyl, 1962-1963 ....45.00-85.00
20" (51cm) nurser, doesn't wet, cryer box, 1968 ....100.00
20" (51cm) dressed in pink, 1985-1986 ....95.00
KITTEN KRIES
    20" (51cm) cloth/vinyl, 1967...100.00
KITTEN, LIVELY 14" (36cm), 18" (46cm) 24" (61cm) knob moves
head and limbs, 1962-1963...150.00 up
KITTEN, MAMA 18" (46cm) same as *Lively* but also has cryer box,
1963...150.00 up
KLONDIKE KATE 10" (25cm) hard plastic, 1963 ....1,050.00
KOREA 8" (20cm) hard plastic, bend knee, 1968-1970 ....225.00
    Re-introduced 1988-1989 ....110.00

This adorable *Littlest Kitten* baby is hard plastic and vinyl in an 8in (20cm) size. She was made in 1963. *Marge Meisinger Collection. Photograph by Michael Cadotte.*

LADY & CHILD, HER
    21" (53cm) porcelain, and
    8" (20cm) hard plastic,
    1993-1994 ....$ 500.00
LADY BIRD 8" (20cm)
    Storyland Dolls,
    1988-1989...............................100.00
LADY BIRD JOHNSON
    14" (36cm) *First Ladies Series*, 1994 ....100.00
LADY HAMILTON 11" (28cm)
    hard plastic, pink silk gown,
    picture hat, 1957..................450.00

Brenda Starr is a famous comic strip character. In another unusual move, Madame Alexander purchased a license and entered the 12in (31cm) fashion doll race. This version is mint in the box and dressed as a bride. She dates from 1964. *Marge Meisinger Collection. Photograph by Michael Cadotte.*

LADY HAMILTON *continued*

20" (51cm) hard plastic/vinyl arms, picture hat, blue gown w/shoulder shawl effect, *Models Formal Series*, 1957......................$ 800.00

21" (53cm) #2182, beige lace over pink gown, 1968.........................500.00

12" (31cm) vinyl, *Portraits of History*, 1984-1986......65.00

LADY IN RED 21" (53cm) red taffeta, 1958.............1,550.00

10" (25cm) *Portrette Series*, 1990 ....85.00

LADY IN WAITING 8" (20cm) hard plastic, 1955................................1,250.00

LADY LEE 8" (20cm) *Storyland Dolls*, 1988 ....90.00

LADY LOVELACE cloth/felt, 1930s 655.00

LADY VALENTINE 8" (20cm) hard plastic, *Storyland Dolls*, 1994 ....55.00

LADY WINDERMERE 21" (53cm) composition, 1945-1946.................1,850.00

LANE, HARRIET 3rd set, *First Ladies Series*, 1982-1984 ....110.00

LAOS 8" (20cm) straight legs, 1987-1988..75.00

LAPLAND 8" (20cm) *International Dolls*, 1993 ....50.00

LATVIA 8" (20cm) straight legs, 1987...75.00

LAUGHING ALLEGRA cloth, 1932..725.00

LAURIE, LITTLE MEN 8" (20cm) hard plastic, bend knee, 1966-1972..150.00

Check pants...65.00

Straight legs, 1973-1975..70.00

Straight legs, 1976-1992..60.00

12" (31cm) all hard plastic, 1966 only 500.00

12" (31cm) plastic/vinyl, 1967-1988 ....75.00

12" (31cm) plastic/vinyl, made for Sears, 1989-1990 *(see Little Women)*

LAZY MARY 7" (18cm) composition, 1936-1938.....................................300.00

LE PETIT BOUDOIR 10" (25cm) Collector's United, 1992

(see Special Dolls) 135.00

LENA *(see River Boat)*

LENNOX, MARY 14" (36cm) *Classic Dolls*, 1993-1994.........................100.00

LESLIE (BLACK POLLY) 17" (43cm) vinyl, in dress, 1965-1971 ....385.00

Ballerina, 1966-1971 ....365.00

Bride, 1966-1971 ....320.00

In formal, 1965-1971 ....485.00

In trunk, wardrobe ....750.00 up

LETTY BRIDESMAID 7-8" (18-20cm) composition, 1938-1940 ....300.00

Ready to walk down the aisle is this wonderful 8in (20cm) all hard plastic *Bride* from 1964-1965. Her *Bridegroom* has been waiting at the altar quite awhile! He is from 1956-1958! Another similar groom was available from 1961-1963. *Marge Meisinger Collection. Photograph by Michael Cadotte.*

LEWIS, SHARI   14" (36cm) 1958-1959 ....$ 775.00
   21" (53cm) 1958-1959 ....995.00
LIESL   *(see Sound of Music)*
'LIL CHRISTMAS COOKIE   8" (20cm) *Americana Series*, 1993-1994 ....55.00
'LIL CLARA & NUTCRACKER   8" (20cm) 1993-1994..............................50.00
'LIL MISS GENIUS   7" (18cm) vinyl, 1993-1994 ....40.00
'LIL SIR GENIUS   7" (18cm) 1993-1994 ....40.00
LILA BRIDESMAID   7-8" (18-20cm) composition, 1938-1940................290.00
LILAC FAIRIE BALLERINA   21" (53cm) plastic/vinyl, *Portrait*,
   1993-1994 ....300.00
LILIBET   16" (41cm) composition, 1938 ....775.00
LILY   10"(25cm) hard plastic, 1987-1988..75.00
LINCOLN, MARY TODD   3rd set, *First Ladies Series*, 1982-1984 ....165.00
LIND, JENNY   10" (25cm) all pink, no trim, *Portrette Series*, 1969 ......700.00
   10" (25cm) hard plastic, pink w/lace trim, *Portrette Series*, 1970...........695.00
   14" (36cm) plastic/vinyl, *Portrait Children Series*, 1970-1971 ....410.00
   21" (53cm) hard plastic/vinyl arms, dressed in all pink, no trim, 1969.......1,225.00
   21" (53cm) plastic/vinyl, all pink w/lace trim, 1970 ....1,325.00
LIND, JENNY & LISTENING CAT   14" (36cm) plastic/vinyl,
   Portrait Children Series, 1970-1971 ....415.00
LION TAMER   8" (20cm) *Americana Series*, 1990 ....80.00
LISSY   11-1/2 - 12" (29-31cm) hard plastic, jointed knees and
   elbows, 1956-1958..310.00
   Ballerina, 1956 and 1958 ....350.00
   Bride, 1956-1958 *(see Lissy under Bride)*...325.00
   Bridesmaid, 1956-1957 ....450.00
   Street dresses, 1956-1958 ....300.00
   Window box w/wardrobe, 1956...1,550.00
   21" (53cm) *Portrait*, pink tiara, 1966 ....1,975.00

The "so called" *Fisher Quints* were manufactured in 1964 only. The box stated that the dolls were made by the manufacturers of the original Quintuplet dolls. Because one doll was dressed in blue, the name was speculative. Extra clothing was also available. *Marge Meisinger Collection.*

LITHUANIA   8" (20cm) hard plastic, *International Series*, 1994 ....$ 50.00
LITTLE ANGEL   9" (23cm) latex/vinyl, 1950-1957..............................195.00
LITTLE BETTY   9-11" (23-28cm) composition, 1935-1943.................295.00
LITTLE BITSEY   9" (23cm) vinyl, nurser, 1967-1968 ....180.00
LITTLE BO PEEP   *(see Bo Peep, Little)*
LITTLE BOY BLUE   7" (18cm) composition, 1937-1939.....................295.00 up
LITTLE BUTCH   9" (23cm) all vinyl nurser, 1967-1968 ....175.00
LITTLE CHERUB   11" (28cm) composition, 1945-1946.........................390.00
   7" (18cm) all vinyl, 1960 ....300.00
LITTLE COLONEL
   8-1/2 - 9" (22-23cm) composition, closed mouth, (rare size)1935 ...825.00
   11-13" (28-33cm) composition, closed mouth 595.00-675.00
   14-17" (36-43cm) composition, open mouth.........................675.00-700.00
   18-23" (46-58cm) composition, open mouth.........................800.00-875.00
   26-27" (66-69cm) composition, open mouth 1,050.00
LITTLE DEVIL   8" (20cm) hard plastic, *Americana Series*, 1992-1993.....55.00
LITTLE DORRIT   16" (41cm) cloth, Dicken's character, early 1930s......725.00
LITTLE EMILY   16" (41cm) cloth, Dicken's character, early 1930s 725.00
LITTLE EMPEROR   8" (20cm) UFDC luncheon, 1992
   (see Special Dolls)...600.00
LITTLE GENIUS   12-14" (31-36cm) composition/cloth, 1935-1940,
   1942-1946...140.00
   18-20" (46-51cm) composition/cloth, 1935-1937,
   1942-1946...160.00-175.00
   24-25" (61-64cm) composition/cloth, 1936-1940 ....175.00-195.00
   8" (20cm) hard plastic/vinyl, undressed, 1956-1962 ....145.00
   Christening outfit 360.00
   Cotton play dress 235.00
   Dressy, lacy outfit w/bonnet 285.00
   7" (18cm) Birthday Party, hard plastic/vinyl, 1994 ....40.00
   7" (18cm) Christening, hard plastic/vinyl, 1994.............................40.00
   7" (18cm) *Genius Elf*, hard plastic/vinyl, 1994 ....40.00
   7" (18cm) *Little Miss Genius*, hard plastic/vinyl, 1993-1994 ....40.00
   7" (18cm) *Little Sir Genius*, hard plastic/vinyl, 1993-1994 ....40.00
   7" (18cm) *Super Genius*, hard plastic/vinyl, 1994...........................40.00
   Sleepy time fashion, 1993-1994...20.00

While dressed dolls were the most desirable, "so called" basic dolls were available dressed in panties, shoes and socks. This particular 8in (20cm) all hard plastic doll is the 1964 version of *Wendy. Marge Meisinger Collection. Photograph by Michael Cadotte.*

LITTLE GENIUS *continued*
Playtime fashion,
1993-1994 ....$ 20.00
Layette fashion,
1993-1994 ....20.00
Beach fashion, 1993 ....20.00
Fashion dress, 1994 ....N/A
LITTLE GODEY 8" (20cm) hard
plastic, 1953-1955 ....985.00 up
LITTLE GRANNY 14" (36cm)
plastic/vinyl, 1966 ....240.00
14" (36cm) pinstripe or floral
gown, 1966 ....245.00
LITTLE HUGGUMS 12" (31cm)
made for I. Magnin, 1992
(see Special Dolls) also *(see Huggums, Little)* 95.00
Baby Bear dress, 12" (31cm), 1994 ....40.00
Christening dress, 12" (31cm), 1993-1994 ....55.00
Christmas, 12" (31cm), 1994 ....50.00
Denton, 12" (31cm), 1993-1994 ....40.00
Dress, 12" (31cm), 1993 ....42.00
Pajamas, 12" (31cm), 1993-1994 ....40.00
Pink check w/hat, 1993-1994 ....45.00
Pink teatime, 12" (31cm), 1993-1994 ....42.00
Sailor suit, 12" (31cm), 1993 ....45.00
LITTLE JACK HORNER 7" (18cm) composition, 1937-1943 ....350.00
LITTLE JUMPING JOAN 8" (20cm) *Storyland Dolls*, 1989-1990 ....90.00
LITTLE LADY DOLL 8" (20cm) hard plastic, gift set, 1960 (mint)....1,250.00
8" (20cm) doll 365.00
21" (53cm) hard plastic, has braids and Colonial gown, 1949......2,100.00
LITTLE LORD FAUNTLEROY 16" (41cm) cloth, 1930s 725.00
13" (33cm) composition, 1936-1937 ....700.00
LITTLE MADELINE 8" (20cm) hard plastic, pink or blue, 1953..........645.00
LITTLE MAID 8" (20cm) straight legs, *Storyland Dolls*, 1987-1988....90.00
LITTLE MELANIE 8" (20cm) hard plastic, 1955-1956 ....975.00 up
LITTLE MEN, (Nat, Stuffy and Tommy Bangs)
15" (38cm) hard plastic, circa 1952 ....855.00 each, 2,500.00 set
LITTLE MERMAID 10" (25cm) hard plastic, *Portrette Series*,
1992-1993..............................105.00
LITTLE MINISTER 8" (20cm) hard plastic, 1957..........................1,550.00 up
LITTLE MISS 8" (20cm) hard plastic, *Storyland Dolls*, 1989-1991......55.00
LITTLE MISS GODEY 8" (20cm) hard plastic, MADC, 1992
(see Special Dolls) 135.00

Collectors love a mystery. On the wall at the Alexander Doll Company is this certificate honoring Madame Alexander for dolls and costumes made from the 1964 movie, *The Fall of the Roman Empire*. Where are these dolls today and what were they? *Photograph Courtesy of Bob Gantz.*

LITTLE MISS MAGNIN
8" (20cm) hard plastic,
I. Magnin, 1991-1992
(see Special Dolls)....$ 90.00
LITTLE MISS MUFFET
8" (20cm) hard plastic,
Storyland Dolls,
1993-1994....................60.00
LITTLE NANNY ETTICOAT
straight legs, *Storyland
Dolls*, 1986-1988..........90.00
LITTLE NELL
16" (41cm) cloth, Dicken's
character, early 1930s 750.00
14" (36cm) composition, 1938-1940 ....700.00
LITTLE SHAVER   7" (18cm) cloth, 1940-1944 ....495.00
10" (25cm) cloth, 1940-1944.....................500.00
15" (38cm) cloth, 1940-1944.....................550.00
22" (56cm) cloth, 1940-1944.....................575.00
12" (31cm) plastic/vinyl, painted eyes, 1963-1965 ....325.00
LITTLE SOUTHERN BOY/GIRL   10" (25cm) latex/vinyl, 1950-1951 ...175.00 each
LITTLE SOUTHERN GIRL   8" (20cm) hard plastic, 1953.................1,000.00
LITTLE VICTORIA   7-1/2 - 8" (19-20cm) 1953-1954.................1,335.00
LITTLE WOMEN   (**Meg, Jo Amy, Beth,** later **Marme or Marmee**)
16" (41cm) cloth, 1930-1936.....................700.00
7" (18cm) composition, 1935-1944 ....300.00 each
9" (23cm) composition, 1937-1940 ....325.00 each
14-15" (36-38cm) hard plastic, 1947-1950.....................450.00 each
14-15" (36-38cm) *Amy* w/loop curls, 1947-1950 ....525.00
14-15" (36-38cm) hard plastic, spread fingers, early 1950s..........425.00 each
matched set ....725.00 each
11-1/2 - 12" (29-31cm) hard plastic, jointed elbow and knees,
1957-1958 ....350.00 each
11-1/2 - 12" (29-31cm) hard plastic, one-piece arms and legs,
1959-1966 ....275.00 each
7-1/2 - 8" (19-20cm) hard plastic, straight leg walker, plus "Marme",
1955 ....325.00 each
8" (20cm) hard plastic, bend knee walker, 1956-1959.....................265.00 each
8" (20cm) bend knee, 1960-1972 ....155.00 each
8" (20cm) straight legs, 1973-1975 ....80.00 each
8" (20cm) straight legs, 1976-1992 ....75.00 each
12"(31cm) plastic/vinyl, 1969-1982.....................80.00 each
12" (31cm) plastic/vinyl, new outfits, 1983-1989 ....65.00 each
12" (31cm) set made for Sears, 1989-1990 *(see Special Dolls)*.....400.00

A beautiful *Wendy* from 1965. This was the last year that the name Wendy would be used on the miniature dolls until the late 1980s. She is an 8in (20cm) all hard plastic doll. *Marge Meisinger Collection. Photograph by Michael Cadotte.*

LITTLE WOMEN
continued
    12" (31cm) hard plastic,
    1993 ....$ 100.00
LITTLEST KITTEN
    8" (20cm) vinyl,
        nude, 1963 ....190.00
    Christening outfit..345.00
    Dressy, lacy outfit and
        bonnet 300.00
    Play outfits...........165.00
LIVELY HUGGUMS
    25" (64cm) knob moves
    limbs and makes
    head move, 1963...100.00
LIVELY KITTEN 14" (36cm),
    18" (46cm), 24" (61cm),
    knob moves limbs and
    makes head turn,
    1962-1963 ....175.00
LIVELY PUSSY CAT
    14" (36cm), 20" (51cm),
24" (61cm), knob moves limbs and makes head move,
1966-1969..125.00
LOLA AND LOLLIE BRIDESMAID 7" (18cm) composition,
1938-1940...400.00
each
LOLLIE BABY rubber/composition, 1941-1942.................................125.00
LORD FAUNTLEROY 12" (31cm) *Portrait Children*, 1981-1983 ....90.00
LORD VALENTINE 8" (20cm) hard plastic, *Storyland Dolls*, 1994.......50.00
LOUISA *(see Sound of Music)*
LOVEY DOVEY 19" (48cm) vinyl baby, closed mouth, molded or
rooted hair, 1958-1959 ....175.00
    12" (31cm) all hard plastic toddler, 1948-1951 ....375.00
    19" (48cm) hard plastic/latex, 1950-1951.......................................225.00
LUCINDA 12" (31cm) plastic/vinyl, 1969-1970 ....360.00
    14" (36cm) plastic/vinyl, blue gown, 1971-1982 ....100.00
    14" (36cm) pink or peach gown, *Classic Dolls*, 1983-1986..............90.00
LUCK OF THE IRISH 8" (20cm) *Americana Series*, 1992-1993.............55.00
LUCY 8" (20cm) hard plastic, *Americana Series*, 1961..................1,225.00
LUCY BRIDE 14" (36cm) composition, 1937-1940...........................400.00
    17" (43cm) composition, 1937-1940...495.00
    14" (36cm) hard plastic, 1949-1950...535.00 up
    17" (43cm) hard plastic, 1949-1950...575.00

A special 8in (20cm) all hard plastic doll is this *Scarlett*. She is mint with her wrist booklet and was made in 1965 only. She is hard to find in this condition. *Marge Meisinger Collection. Photograph by Michael Cadotte.*

MADAME (ALEXANDER)
21" (53cm) one-piece
  skirt in pink,
  1984............$ 425.00
21" (53cm) pink w/
  overskirt,
  1985-1987.......390.00
21" (53cm) blue w/
  full lace overskirt,
  1988-1990.......345.00
MADAME BUTTERFLY
10" (25cm) made for
Marshall Fields, 1990 *(see Special Dolls)*...............................95.00-100.00
MADAME DOLL 21" (53cm) hard plastic/vinyl arms, pink
brocade, 1966 only...2,350.00
  14" (36cm) plastic/vinyl, *Classic Dolls*, 1967-1975....................225.00 up
MADAME POMPADOUR 21" (53cm) hard plastic/vinyl arms,
pink lace overskirt, 1970...1,250.00
MADELAINE 14" (36cm) composition, 1940..565.00
  8" (20cm) hard plastic, FAO Schwarz special, 1954.........................800.00
  17-18" (43-46cm) hard plastic, 1949-1952.....................................765.00
MADELAINE DU BAIN 11" (28cm) composition, closed mouth, 1937.....500.00
  14" (36cm) composition, 1938-1939...500.00
  17" (43cm) composition, 1939-1941...625.00
  21" (53cm) composition, 1939-1941...800.00
  14" (36cm) hard plastic, 1949-1951..985.00
MADELINE 17-18" (43-46cm) hard plastic, jointed elbows and
  knees, 1950-1953..575.00
  18" (46cm) hard plastic/vinyl head, jointed body, 1961....................815.00
MADISON, DOLLY 1st set, *First Ladies Series*, 1976-1978..................140.00
MAGGIE 15" (38cm) hard plastic, 1948-1952.....................................500.00
  17-18" (43-46cm) hard plastic, 1949-1952.....................................655.00
  20-21" (51-53cm) hard plastic, 1948-1952.....................................685.00
  22-23" (56-58cm) hard plastic, 1949-1952.....................................780.00
  17" (43cm) plastic/vinyl, 1972-1973..195.00
MAGGIE MIXUP 8" (20cm) hard plastic, 1960-1961.............................445.00
  8" (20cm) in riding habit, 1960-1961..575.00
  8" (20cm) in skater outfit, 1960-1961...575.00
  8" (20cm) hard plastic, Angel, 1961...700.00

James Whitcomb Riley's poem, "Little Orphant Annie," delighted Madame Alexander so much, she designed this delicate 14in (36cm) doll in vinyl and hard plastic issued in 1965-1966. The doll came with the poem. *Marge Meisinger Collection. Photograph by Michael Cadotte.*

MAGGIE MIXUP *continued*
   8" (20cm) in overalls, watering
     can, 1961 ....$ 675.00
   17" (43cm) plastic/vinyl,
     1960-1961..........................400.00
MAGGIE TEENAGER
   15-18" (38-46cm) hard plastic,
     1951-1952..........................550.00
   23" (58cm) 1951-1953 ....700.00
MAGGIE WALKER
   15-18" (38-46cm) hard plastic,
     1949-1952..........................425.00
   20-21" (51-53cm) 1949-1952...575.00
   23-25" (58-64cm) 1951-1952..650.00
MAGNOLIA 21" (53cm) rows of lace
   on pink gown, 1977..........525.00
   21" (53cm) yellow gown,
     1988 ....275.00
MAID MARIAN 8" (20cm) hard plastic,
   Storyland Dolls, 1989-1991...60.00
   21" (53cm) *Portrait Series*,
     1993 ....300.00
MAID OF HONOR 18" (46cm)
composition, 1940-1944 ....750.00
   14" (36cm) plastic/vinyl, *Classic Dolls*, 1988-1989 ....85.00
MAJORETTE 14-17" (36-43cm) composition, 1937-1938......................900.00
   8" (20cm) hard plastic, 1955 ....725.00
   8" (20cm) *Americana Series*, 1991-1992..55.00
MAMMY 8" (20cm) Jubilee II set, 1989..90.00
   8" (20cm) hard plastic, *Scarlett Series*, 1991-1992........................55.00
MANET 21" (53cm) light brown w/dark brown pinstripes, 1982-1983 .....225.00
   14" (36cm) *Fine Arts Series*, 1986-1987..75.00
MARCH HARE cloth/felt, mid-1930s..800.00
MARDI GRAS 10" (25cm) made for Spiegel, 1992 *(see Special Dolls)* 110.00
MARGARET ROSE *(see Princess)*
MARGOT 10" (25cm) hard plastic, formals, 1961 ....470.00
   Street dresses, bathing suit, 1961 ....325.00
MARGOT BALLERINA 15-18" (38-46cm) 1953-1955 ....500.00
   15-18" (38-46cm) hard plastic/vinyl arms, 1955 ....365.00
MARIA *(see Sound of Music)*
MARIE ANTOINETTE 21" (53cm) composition, *Portrait Series*, 1940s ...1,550.00
   21" (53cm) floral print w/pink insert, 1987-1988 ....285.00
MARINE (BOY) 14" (36cm) composition, 1943-1944..............................800.00
MARIONETTES, TONY SARG composition, 1934-1940 ....295.00
   12" (31cm) composition, made for Disney World® 350.00
MARME *(see Little Women)*
MARTA *(see Sound of Music)*

The *Americana Series* included this 8in (20cm) all hard plastic set of *Amish Boy* and *Girl*, available from 1966-1969. These dolls are often found in Pennsylvania, where dealers ordered more heavily. *Marge Meisinger Collection. Photograph by Michael Cadotte.*

MARTIN, MARY
14-17"
(36-43cm)
hard plastic,
formal, 1948-1951 ....$800.00-1,000.00
   14-17" (36-43cm) in sailor suit, 1948-1951 ....900.00-1,100.00
MARY ANN 14" (36cm) plastic/vinyl, ballerina, 1965 ....245.00
   Assorted outfits 225.00
   14" (36cm) hard plastic/vinyl, *Classic Dolls*, 1994 ....100.00
MARYBEL 16" (41cm) rigid vinyl, *The Doll Who Gets Well*, 1959-1965
   In case, 1959, 1961, 1965...400.00
   In case w/wardrobe, 1960..425.00
   In case, w/long, straight hair, 1965..500.00
MARY CASSATT BABY
   14" (36cm) cloth/vinyl, 1969-1970 ....185.00
   14" (36cm) plastic/vinyl child, *Fine Arts Series*, 1987 ....100.00
   20" (51cm) 1969-1970..250.00
MARY ELLEN 31" (79cm) hard plastic, 1954...................................625.00
   31" (79cm) plastic/vinyl arms, jointed elbows, 1955.......................485.00
MARY ELLEN PLAYMATE 16" (41cm) plastic/vinyl,
Marshall Fields exclusive, 1965 ....350.00
   12" (31cm) in case w/wigs, 1965 ....725.00
MARY GRAY 14" (36cm) plastic/vinyl, *Classic Dolls*, 1988 ....90.00
MARY LOUISE 8" (20cm) hard plastic, same as 18" (46cm) *Me
and My Shadow Series*, 1954 ....1,000.00 up
   18" (46cm) hard plastic, orange and green, *Me and My Shadow
Series*, 1954 ....1,250.00
MARY, MARY 8" (20cm) hard plastic, bend knee, *Storyland Dolls*,
1965-1972..155.00
   8" (20cm) hard plastic, straight legs, 1973-1975 ....75.00
   8" (20cm) hard plastic, straight legs, 1976-1987 ....70.00
   8" (20cm) hard plastic, re-introduced 1992-1993 ....55.00
   14" (36cm) plastic/vinyl, *Classic Dolls*, 1988-1990 ....75.00
   14" (36cm) plastic/vinyl, *Classic Dolls*, 1994...............................100.00
MARY MINE 21" (53cm) cloth/vinyl, 1977-1989 ....145.00
   14" (36cm) cloth/vinyl, 1977-1979 ....95.00
   14" (36cm) re-introduced 1989 ....60.00

To celebrate the joining of the state of Hawaii to the U.S., the Alexander Doll company issued this fantastic 8in (20cm) dark skinned all hard plastic doll in 1966-1969. *Marge Meisinger Collection. Photograph by Michael Cadotte.*

MARY MUSLIN 19" (48cm) cloth, 1951 ....$ 677.00
    26" (66cm) 1951....800.00
    40" (101cm) 1951..1,000.00
MARY, QUEEN OF SCOTS 21" (53cm) 1988-1989.....350.00
MARY ROSE BRIDE
    17" (43cm) hard plastic, 1951 ....600.00 up
MARY SUNSHINE
    15" (38cm) plastic/vinyl, 1961 ....385.00
MAYOR OF MUNCHKINLAND
    8" (20cm) hard plastic, *Wizard of Oz Series*, 1994 ....55.00
MCELROY, MARY
    4th set, *First Ladies Series*, 1985-1987 ...100.00
MCGUFFEY ANA
    16" (41cm) cloth, 1934-1936 ....725.00
    7" (18cm) composition, 1935-1939 ....350.00

9" (23cm) composition, 1935-1939..400.00
11" (28cm) closed mouth, 1937-1939 ....650.00
11-13" (28-33cm) composition, 1937-1944 ....600.00-700.00
13" (33cm) composition, 1938 ....700.00
14-16" (36-41cm) composition, 1937-1944.........................525.00-625.00
14-1/2" (37cm) composition, coat, hat and muff, 1948 ....750.00
15" (38cm) composition, 1935-1937..700.00
17" (43cm) composition, 1948-1949..825.00
17-20" (43-51cm) composition, 1937-1943.........................725.00-850.00
21-25" (53-64cm) composition, 1937-1942.........................800.00-950.00
28" (71cm) composition, 1937-1939..1,020.00
8" (20cm) hard plastic, 1956 ....675.00
18" (46cm), 25" (64cm), 31" (79cm) flat feet, 1955-1956....510.00-825.00
21" (53cm) hard plastic, 1948-1950..875.00
8" (20cm) hard plastic, was *American Girl* in 1962-1963, 1964-1965..400.00
14" (36cm) plastic/vinyl, plaid dress, eyelet apron, *Classic Dolls*, 1968-1969 ....150.00
14" (36cm) plastic/vinyl, plaid dress, *Classic Dolls*, 1977-1986.......125.00
14" (36cm) plastic/vinyl, mauve stripe pinafore, *Classic Dolls*, 1987-1988..70.00

Marshall Fields featured this 16in (41cm) *Mary Ellen Playmate* made of vinyl and hard plastic in 1966. The same doll was used for *Polly* as well. *Marge Meisinger Collection. Photograph by Michael Cadotte.*

McGuffey Ana

continued

8" (20cm) *Storyland Dolls,* 1990-1991.$ 55.00
21" (31cm) hard plastic, very rare doll, 1963......1,225.00 up

McKee, Mary

4th set, *First Ladies Series,* 1985-1987.......90.00

McKinley, Ida

5th set, *First Ladies Series,* 1988..............100.00

Medici, Catherine De   21" (53cm) porcelain, 1990-1991.................525.00
Meg *(see Little Women)*
Melanie 8" (20cm) hard plastic, 1955-1956.....................1,050.00
  21" (53cm) hard plastic/vinyl arms, lace bodice and
    overdress over satin, 1961 ....750.00
  21" (53cm) blue gown, wide lace down sides, 1966 ....2,350.00
  10" (25cm) pink multi-tiered skirt, 1969 ....450.00
  10" (25cm) yellow multi-tiered skirt, 1970 ....450.00
  21" (53cm) blue, white rick-rack around hem ruffle, blonde, 1967 .....525.00
  21" (53cm) rust faille gown, braid trim, brown velvet hat, 1968......575.00
  21" (53cm) blue gown, white trim, multi-rows of lace, bonnet, 1969.....525.00
  21" (53cm) white gown, red ribbon trim, 1970 ....575.00
  21" (553cm) blue gown, white sequin trim, 1971 ....475.00
  21" (53cm) white gown, red jacket and bonnet, 1974 ....520.00
  21" (53cm) white nylon gown w/pink trim, 1979-1980 ....365.00
  21" (53cm) pink nylon w/blue ribbon, 1981.........................325.00
  12" (31cm) green gown, brown trim, *Portrait Children Series,* 1987 ....95.00
  10" (25cm) all royal blue, black trim, *Jubilee II,* 1989 ....85.00
  8" (20cm) lavender, lace, *Scarlett Series,* 1990.................65.00
  8" (20cm) peach gown, bonnet w/lace, 1992........................57.00
  21" (53cm) all orange w/lace shawl, 1989.........................300.00
Melinda   10" (25cm) hard plastic, blue gown w/white trim, 1968 ....375.00
  10" (25cm) yellow multi-tiered lace skirt, 1970.................365.00
  14" (36cm), 16" (41cm), 22" (56cm) plastic/vinyl, 1963.......275.00-455.00 up
  14" (36cm) ballerina, 1963 ....355.00
  16-22" (41-56cm) plastic/vinyl, 1962-1963.......................380.00

To help celebrate the state of Alaska joining the Union, the Alexander Doll Company made this delightful *Eskimo* in a (20cm) all hard plastic size. He came with both the smile face and the regular face and was available 1966-1969. *Marge Meisinger Collection. Photograph by Michael Cadotte.*

MELODY AND FRIEND
    8" (20cm) hard plastic,
    Alexander and 26" (66cm)
    porcelain, Günzel, 1991
    (see Special Dolls).......$ 850.00
MERRY ANGEL 8" (20cm)
    made for Spiegel, 1991
    (see Special Dolls)..........125.00
MEXICO
    7" (18cm) composition,
      1936...........................290.00
    9" (23cm) composition,
      1938-1939....................310.00
    8" (20cm) hard plastic, bend
  knee walker, 1964-1965 ....169.00
  8" (20cm) hard plastic, bend knee, 1965-1972 ....135.00
  8" (20cm) straight legs, 1973-1975...75.00
  8" (20cm) straight legs, 1976-1991 ....45.00
MICHAEL 11" (28cm) plastic/vinyl, w/teddy bear,
  1969 (*Peter Pan* set) 400.00
  8" (20cm) *Storyland Dolls*, 1992-1993....................................52.00
MIDNIGHT 21" (53cm) dark blue, black, 1990 ....250.00
MIMI 30" (76cm) multi-jointed body, in formal, 1961 ....900.00
  Red sweater, plaid skirt..475.00
  Romper suit, skirt..475.00
  Slacks, stripe top, straw hat...475.00
  Tyrolean outfit 925.00
  14" (36cm) *Opera Series*, 1983-1986 ....90.00
  21" (53cm) hard plastic/vinyl arms, pink cape and trim on
    white gown, *Portrait Series*, 1971.......................................600.00
MISS AMERICA 14" (36cm) composition, 1941-1943.............................800.00
MISS LEIGH 8" (20cm) CU Gathering, 1989 *(see Special Dolls)* 200.00
MISS LIBERTY 10" (25cm) MADC, 1991 *(see Special Dolls)* 125.00
MISS MAGNIN 10" (25cm) made for I. Magnin, 1991 *(see Special Dolls)*.....125.00
MISS MUFFETT 8" (20cm) hard plastic, bend knee, *Storyland Dolls*,
  1965-1972...148.00
  8" (20cm) straight legs, 1973-1975...75.00
  8" (20cm) straight legs, 1976-1986...70.00
  8" (20cm) straight legs, 1987-1988...65.00

What collector would not go insane over this display house full of 1966 21in (53cm) Portrait dolls. Featuring the ethereal *Coco* doll face and body, offered in 1966 only, these dolls are any collector's dream come true. *Alexander Doll Company. Photograph Courtesy of Bob Gantz.*

Miss Scarlett
14" (36cm) plastic/vinyl, made
for Belk & Leggett, 1988
(see Special Dolls).............$ 110.00
Miss Unity
10" (25cm) hard plastic,
UFDC, 1991 *(see Special Dolls)*.....................................300.00
Miss U.S.A.
8" (20cm) hard plastic, bend knee,
Americana Series,
1966-1968..............................335.00
Miss Victory
20" (51cm) composition, magnetic
hands, 1944-1946.....................800.00
Mistress Mary
7" (18cm) composition,
1937-1941...285.00
Molly 14" (36cm) *Classic Dolls*, 1988 ....75.00
Molly Cottontail cloth/felt, 1930s 655.00
Mombo 8" (20cm) hard plastic, *Wendy Loves the Mombo*, 1955......675.00
Mommy and Me 14" (36cm) and 9" (23cm) composition,
matching outfits, 1940-1943...1,565.00 set
Mommy's Pet 14-20" (36-51cm) cloth/vinyl, 1977-1986.........55.00-70.00
Monet 21" (53cm) hard plastic, black and white check gown
w/red jacket, 1984-1985 ....310.00
Monique 8" (2cm) hard plastic, Disneyland® Teddy Bear &
Classic Dolls, 1993 *(see Special Dolls)* 525.00
Monroe, Elizabeth 1st set, *First Ladies Series*, 1976-1978 ....135.00
Mop Top Billy 8" (20cm) hard plastic, *Storyland Dolls*, 1994 ....55.00
Mop Top Wendy 8" (20cm) hard plastic, *Storyland Dolls*, 1994........55.00
Morisot 21" (53cm) plastic/vinyl, lime green gown
w/white lace, 1985-1986 ....225.00
Morocco 8" (20cm) hard plastic, bend knee, 1968-1970 ....385.00
Moss Rose 14" (36cm) *Classic Dolls*, 1991....................................165.00
Mother Goose 8" (20cm) straight legs, *Storyland Dolls*, 1986-1992 ....65.00
Mother Hubbard 8" (20cm) *Storyland Dolls*, 1988-1989.................65.00
Mouseketeer 8" (20cm) made for Disney®, 1991 *(see Special Dolls)* 95.00
Mr. O'Hara 8" (20cm) *Scarlett Series*, 1993 ....53.00
Mrs. Buck Rabbit cloth/felt, mid-1930s...650.00
Mrs. Claus 8" (20cm) mid-year release, 1993.................................75.00
Mrs. March Hare cloth/felt, mid-1930s 650.00
Mrs. Molloy's Millinery Shop 10" (25cm) *Portrette* trunk set, 1994...190.00
Mrs. O'Hara 8" (20cm) *Scarlett* Series, 1992-1993 ....57.00

The 1966 movie, *The Sound of Music*, inspired Madame Alexander to design two sets of dolls. Featured here on a company publicity photo is the larger set. *Alexander Doll Company. Photograph Courtesy of Bob Gantz.*

MRS. QUACK-A-FIELD
cloth/felt, mid-1930s
..........................$ 675.00

MRS. SNOOPIE
cloth/felt,
1940s....................675.00

MUFFIN 19" (48cm)
cloth, 1966........150.00
14" (36cm)
1963-1977.........125.00
12" (31cm) all
vinyl, 1989-1990
..........................60.00
12" (31cm) in trunk,
wardrobe,
1990-1991........150.00

MUNCHKIN HERALD
8" (20cm) hard plastic,
Wizard of Oz Series,
1994.....................55.00

MUNCHKIN PEASANT 8" (20cm) hard plastic, *Wizard of Oz Series,*
1994..55.00

MY LITTLE SWEETHEART white and black, made for *A Child at Heart*, 1992 *(see Special Dolls)*..95.00 up

N

NAN MCDARE cloth/felt, 1940s...$ 700.00
NANA GOVERNESS 8" (20cm) hard plastic, 1957 ....1,250.00 up
NANA STORYLAND (stuffed dog) 1993 only 40.00
NANCY DAWSON 8" (20cm) hard plastic, *Storyland Dolls*, 1988-1989..95.00
NANCY DREW 12" (31cm) plastic/vinyl, *Literature Series*, 1967........425.00
NANCY JEAN 8" (20cm) hard plastic, made for Belk & Leggett,
1990 *(see Special Dolls)*..75.00
NAPOLEON 12" (31cm) plastic/vinyl, *Portraits of History,* 1980-1986 .....75.00
NATASHA 21" (53cm) brown and paisley brocade, 1989-1990...........345.00
NATIONAL VELVET 12" (31cm) plastic/vinyl, *Romance Series*, 1991 ......80.00
NEIMAN MARCUS 8" (20cm) hard plastic, party trunk, 1990
(see Special Dolls)..300.00

Part of the *Americana Series*, this dazzling *Cowboy* and *Cowgirl* were 8in (20cm) hard plastic dolls. He dates from 1967-1969. She was available 1966-1970. These are personal favorites! *Marge Meisinger Collection. Photograph by Michael Cadotte.*

NELSON, LORD
   12" (31cm)
   plastic, vinyl,
   *Portraits of
   History*,
   1984-
   1986....$ 75.00
**NETHERLAND
BOY**
   Formerly Dutch.
   8" (20cm)
      hard plastic,
      straight legs, 1974-1975 ....75.00
   8" (20cm) hard plastic, straight legs, 1976-1989................................55.00
NETHERLAND GIRL   8" (20cm) hard plastic, 1974-1992.........................55.00
NICOLE   10" (25cm) hard plastic, *Portrette Series*, 1989-1990.............70.00
NIGHTINGALE, FLORENCE   14" (36cm) *Classic Dolls*, 1986-1987.........60.00
NINA BALLERINA   7" (18cm) composition, 1940 ....310.00
   9" (23cm) composition, 1939-1941 ....365.00
   14" (36cm) hard plastic, 1949-1950 ....560.00
   15" (38cm) hard plastic, 1951..625.00
   17" (43cm) hard plastic, 1949-1950 ....545.00
   19" (48cm) hard plastic, 1949-1950 ....675.00
   23" (58cm) hard plastic, 1951..800.00
NOEL   12" (31cm) porcelain, New England Collector's Society,
   1989-1991 *(see Special Dolls)*...200.00 up
NORMANDY   7" (18cm) composition, 1935-1938................................285.00
NORWAY   8" (20cm) hard plastic, bend knee, 1968-1972 ....150.00
   8" (20cm) straight legs, 1973-1975 ....75.00
   8" (20cm) straight legs, 1976-1987 ....65.00
NORWEGIAN   7-8" (18-20cm) composition, 1936-1940.......................295.00
   9" (23cm) composition, 1938-1939 ....320.00
NURSE   7" (18cm) composition, 1936-1939 ....300.00
   13" (33cm) composition, Dionne nurse, 1936................................600.00 up
   8" (20cm) hard plastic, all white, no baby, bend knee walker,
      1956-1957 ....550.00 up
   8" (20cm) w/baby, stripe dress and pinafore, bend knee walker,
      1961-1965 ....485.00 up
   8" (20cm) hard plastic, blue, white striped dress, white pinafore
      and cap, *Americana Series*, 1990 ....60.00
   8" (20cm) hard plastic, white uniform, *Americana Series*, 1991 ....60.00
(see Red Cross Nurse for additional listings)   95

Frances Cavanah's book, *The Secret of Madame Doll*, inspired a delightful 14in (36cm) vinyl and hard plastic doll made from 1967-1975. Earlier editions came with the secret jewelry, but the Company, fearful of injury to a child, discontinued them. The wrist tag told the story of a doll used to save family heirlooms during the Revolutionary War. *Marge Meisinger Collection. Photograph by Michael Cadotte.*

O'BRIEN, MARGARET
14-1/2" (37cm) composition,
1946-1947 ....$ 800.00
18" (46cm), 21" (53cm)
composition,
1946-1947 .....900.00-1,000.00
21-24" (53-61cm)
composition,
1946-1947..1,000.00-1,275.00
14-1/2" (37cm) hard plastic,
1948-1951 ....925.00 up
18" (46cm) hard plastic,
1948-1951 ....1,100.00 up
22" (56cm) hard plastic,
1948-1951 (very rare) 1,350.00 up
OKTOBERFEST
8" (20cm) Greenville Show,
1992 *(see Special Dolls)* .150.00
OKTOBERFEST (BOY) 8" (20cm)
Greenville Show, 1992
(see Special Dolls) 150.00

OLD FASHIONED GIRL
13" (33cm) composition, 1945-1947 ....465.00
14" (36cm) hard plastic, 1948...700.00
20" (51cm) hard plastic, 1948...745.00
OLIVER TWIST 16" (41cm) cloth, Dicken's character, 1934 ....700.00
7" (18cm) composition, 1935-1936 ....325.00
8" (20cm) *Storyland Dolls*, 1992 ....50.00
OLIVER TWISTAIL cloth/felt, 1930s...785.00
OPENING NIGHT 10" (25cm) *Portrette*, 1989...75.00
OPHELIA 12" (31cm) *Romance Collection*, 1992-1993......................115.00
ORPHANT ANNIE 14" (36cm) plastic/vinyl, *Literature Series*,
1965-1966 ....365.00
1965 gift set..500.00 up

The television show "That Girl" was the inspiration for this 17in (43cm) vinyl and hard plastic doll of the actress Marlo Thomas, made in 1967 only. Besides this version, another doll was manufactured in a green and white striped jersey minidress with fishnet stockings and go-go boots. Both are very hard to find today. *Marge Meisinger Collection. Photograph by Michael Cadotte.*

PAKISTAN
8" (20cm) hard plastic, *International Dolls*,
1993...$ 50.00 up
PAMELA 12" (31cm) hard plastic, w/wigs,
window box, 1963...........................500.00 up
In case, 1962-1963..........................950.00 up
12" vinyl head editions, in case,
late 1960s......................................545.00 up
PAMELA PLAYS DRESS UP AT GRANDMA'S
12" (31cm) hard plastic, made for Horchow,
1993 *(see Special Dolls)*.........................250.00
PAN AMERICAN-POLLERA
7" (18cm) composition, 1936-1938......325.00
PANAMA
8" (20cm) hard plastic, 1985-1987......100.00
PANDORA 8" (20cm) hard plastic, made for
Dolls 'n Bearland, 1991
(see Special Dolls).................................95.00
PARLOUR MAID 8" (20cm) hard plastic,
1956...985.00 up
PAT NIXON 14" (36cm) *First Ladies Series*,
1994...100.00
PATCHITY PAM & PEPPER
15" (38cm) cloth, 1965-1966................200.00

PATTERSON, MARTHA JOHNSON 3rd set, *First Ladies Series*, 1982-1984 ...110.00
PATTY 18" (46cm) plastic/vinyl, 1965...245.00
PATTY PIGTAILS 14" (36cm) hard plastic, 1949...................................700.00
PAULETTE 10" (25cm) *Portrette*, 1989-1990..90.00
PEARL (JUNE) 10" (25cm) *Birthstone Collection*, 1992 ....75.00
PEASANT 7" (18cm) composition, 1936-1937 ....290.00
9" (23cm) composition, 1938-1939 ....315.00
PEGGY BRIDE 14-18" (36-46cm) hard plastic, 1950-1951 ....600.00 up
21" (53cm) hard plastic, 1950..800.00
PENNY 7" (18cm) composition, 1938-1940 ....300.00
34" (86cm) cloth/vinyl, 1951 ....500.00
42" (106cm) 1951..650.00
PERSIA 7" (18cm) composition, 1936-1938 ....325.00
PERU 8" (20cm) 1985-1987 ....110.00
8" (20cm) *International Dolls*, 1992-1993 ....50.00
PERUVIAN BOY 8" (20cm) hard plastic, bend knee, 1965-1966 ....425.00
8" (20cm) hard plastic, bend knee walker 500.00
PETER PAN 8" (20cm) hard plastic, *Quiz-Kins*, 1953.....................1,250.00
15" (38cm) hard plastic, 1953..840.00
14" (36cm) plastic/vinyl, 1969...350.00

Made from 1967-1977 as a Disneyland®/Walt Disney World® Exclusive, this 14in (36cm) vinyl doll and features the licensed *Snow White* movie costume. *Marge Meisinger Collection. Photograph by Michael Cadotte.*

PETER PAN *continued*
8" (20cm) hard plastic, *Storyland Dolls*, re-introduced 1991-1994 ....$ 47.00
Complete set of four dolls (**Peter, Michael, Wendy, Tinkerbell**), 1969 ...1,000.00 up
PHILIPPINES 8" (20cm) straight legs, 1985-1987..85.00
yellow gown, 1987 ....125.00
PIERCE, JANE 3rd set, *First Ladies Series*, 1982-1984 ......110.00
PIERROT CLOWN 8" (20cm) hard plastic, 1956 ....975.00 up
14" (36cm) *Classic Dolls*, 1991-1992 ....80.00
PILGRIM 7" (18cm) composition, 1935-1938 ....300.00
8" (20cm) hard plastic, *Americana Series*, 1994 ....47.00
PINK CHAMPAGNE 18" (46cm) hard plastic, 1950 ....3,100.00 up
PINKY 16" (41cm) cloth, 1940s 500.00
23" (58cm) composition, cloth baby, 1937-1939............................275.00
13-19" (33-48cm) vinyl baby, 1954.....................................80.00-100.00
12" (31cm) plastic/vinyl, *Portrait Children Series*, 1975-1987 ....75.00
PINOCCHIO 8" (20cm) *Storyland Dolls*, 1992-1994 ....55.00
PIP all cloth, Dicken's character, early 1930s................................900.00
7" (18cm) composition, 1935-1936 ....325.00
PITTY PAT 16" (41cm) cloth, 1950s...500.00
PITTY PAT CLOWN 1950s.........................455.00
PLAYMATES 29" (74cm) cloth, 1940s....485.00
POCAHONTAS 8" (20cm) hard plastic, bend knee, *Americana* and *Storyland Dolls*, 1967-1970.............................400.00
8" (20cm) hard plastic, *Americana Series*, re-introduced 1991-1992......................52.00
8" (20cm) hard plastic, *Americana Series*, complete costume change, 1994.........45.00
POLISH (POLAND) 7" (18cm) composition, 1935-1936..............................275.00
8" (20cm) hard plastic, bend knee walker, 1964-1965.......................................225.00

This exclusive outfit was made for a 14in (36cm) doll and was tagged *Cinderella*, stock number 140. It was made in 1968 only for FAO Schwarz. *Marge Meisinger Collection. Photograph by Michael Cadotte.*

At the request of a west coast Alexander Doll Company salesman, Frank Martin, about three hundred each of these Easter dolls were made in an 8in (20cm) and a 14in (36cm) size in 1968. Some remained on shelves for years! *Marge Meisinger Collection. Photograph by Michael Cadotte.*

POLISH (POLAND)
    8" (20cm) hard plastic, bend knee, 1965-1972......$ 155.00
    8" (20cm) hard plastic, straight legs, 1973-1975............75.00
    8" (20cm) hard plastic, straight legs, 1976-1988............62.00
    8" (20cm) hard plastic, re-introduced 1992-1994............65.00

POLK, SARAH
    2nd set, *First Ladies Series*, 1979-1981 . . . . 125.00

POLLERA (PAN AMERICAN)   7" (18cm) composition, 1936-1937. . . . . . . 300.00

POLLY   17" (43cm) plastic/vinyl, 1965 . . . . 355.00
    plastic/vinyl, Ballerina 325.00
    plastic/vinyl, Ball gown 460.00
    plastic/vinyl, Bride 365.00
    plastic/vinyl, Street dress 350.00
    plastic/vinyl, in Trunk, wardrobe, 1965. . . . . 900.00

POLLY FLINDERS   8" (20cm) *Storyland Dolls*, 1988-1989 . . . . 115.00

POLLY PIGTAILS   14" (36cm) hard plastic, 1949-1951 . . . . 500.00
    17" (43cm) 1949-1951 . . . . 665.00
    8" (20cm) hard plastic, MADC, 1990 *(see Special Dolls)* 175.00

POLLY PUT THE KETTLE ON   7" (18cm) composition, 1937-1939 . . . . 295.00

POLLYANA   16" (41cm) rigid vinyl, 1960-1961 . . . . 365.00
    22" (56cm) 1960-1961 . . . . 475.00
    14" (36cm) *Classic Dolls*, 1987-1988. . . . . 75.00
    8" (20cm) *Storyland Dolls*, 1992-1993 . . . . 65.00
    14" (36cm) *Classic Dolls*, 1994 . . . . 100.00

One of the most beautiful 21in (53cm) Portrait dolls ever, is this 1969 only Jenny Lind, that features a dress with paniers on each side of the waist. *Marge Meisinger Collection. Photograph by Michael Cadotte.*

POODLE 14-17" (36-43cm) stuffed animal, 1940s ....$ 285.00

PORTRAIT ELISE 17" (43cm) plastic/ vinyl, 1972-1973 ....250.00

PORTUGAL 8" (20cm) hard plastic, bend knee, 1968-1972...............150.00

8" (20cm) straight legs, 1973-197575.00

8" (20cm) straight legs, 1976-198772.00

8" (20cm) *International Dolls*, 1993-1994 ....47.00

POSEY PETS 15" (38cm) cloth, plush animals, 1940s....................435.00

PRECIOUS 12" (31cm) composition/ cloth baby, 1937-1940 ....245.00

12" (31cm) all hard plastic toddler, 1948-195 ....400.00

PRINCE CHARLES 8" (20cm) hard plastic, 1957 ....800.00

PRINCE CHARMING 16-17" (41-43cm) composition, 1947.....................700.00

14-15" (36-38cm) hard plastic, 1948-1950.....................................795.00

17-18" (43-46cm) hard plastic, 1948-1950.....................................910.00

21" (53cm) hard plastic, 1949-1951 ....1,000.00

12" (31cm) hard plastic, *Romance Collection*, 1990-1991.....................90.00

8" (20cm) *Storyland Dolls*, 1993-1994..................70.00

PRINCE PHILLIP
18" (46cm) hard plastic, 1953...........................800.00

21" (53cm) 1953..........900.00

PRINCESS
14" (36cm) plastic/vinyl, 1990-1991.................140.00

12" (31cm) plastic/vinyl, *Romance Collection*, 1990-1992..................92.00

PRINCESS ALEXANDRIA
24" (61cm) cloth, compo- sition, 1937.............250.00 up

PRINCESS AND THE PEA
8" (20cm) hard plastic, made for Dolly Dears, 1993 *(see Special Dolls)*........80.00

Lucky indeed is the collector who owns this alluring Peter Pan Set from 1969. Included are a 14in (36cm) *Peter Pan* and *Wendy*, a 12in (31cm) *Michael and his bear*, and a 10in (25cm) *Tinkerbelle*. For a time, *Tinkerbelle* was sold separately in both a rare 8in (20cm) and the more familiar 10in (25cm) size. *Marge Meisinger Collection. Photograph by Michael Cadotte.*

The *Portrait Series* offered this radiant *Bride* in a 21in (53cm) vinyl and hard plastic in 1969, stock number 2192. *Marge Meisinger Collection. Photograph by Michael Cadotte.*

PRINCESS ANN
  8" (20cm) hard plastic,
  1957......................$ 860.00
PRINCESS BUDDIR-AL-BUDDOOR
  8" (20cm) *Storyland Dolls*,
  1993-1994...................70.00
PRINCESS DOLL
  13-15" (33-38cm)
    composition, 1940-1942 ....565.00
  24" (61cm) composition, 1940-1942 ....815.00
PRINCESS ELIZABETH
  7" (18cm) composition, 1937-1939 ....400.00
  8" (20cm) with Dionne head, 1937 (rare)..425.00
  9-11" (23-28cm) composition,1937-1941.............................385.00-450.00
  13" (33cm) composition w/closed mouth, 1937-1941.......................550.00
  14" (36cm) composition, 1937-1941 ....545.00
  15" (38cm) composition, open mouth, 1937-1941 ....560.00
  18-19" (46-48cm) composition, open mouth, 1937-1941................675.00
  24" (61cm) composition, open mouth, 1938-1939 ....800.00
  28" (71cm) composition, open mouth, 1938-1939 ....995.00
PRINCESS FLAVIA 21" (53cm) composition, 1939, 1946-1947.........1,900.00 up
PRINCESS MARGARET ROSE 15-18" (38-46cm) composition,
  1946-1947 ....650.00 up
  21" (53cm) composition, 1946-1947 ....1,000.00
  14-18-21" (36-46-53cm) hard plastic, 1947-1950.............800.00-1,000.00
  18" (46cm) hard plastic, pink taffeta gown and tiara,
    Beaux Art Series, 1953...1,375.00
PRINCESS ROSETTA 21" (53cm) composition, 1939, 1946-1947......1,600.00
PRISCILLA 18" (46cm) cloth, mid-1930s...700.00
  7" (18cm) composition, 1935-1938 ....310.00
  8" (20cm) hard plastic, bend knee, *Americana* and
    Storyland Dolls, 1965-1970..400.00
PRISSY
  8" (20cm) *Scarlett Series*, 1990..57.00
  8" (20cm) re-introduced 1992-1993..50.00

The book by Frances Cavanah inspired this wonderful 14in (36cm) vinyl and hard plastic *Jenny Lind* and her listening cat. Made from 1970-1971, this doll is a collector's favorite. *Marge Meisinger Collection. Photograph by Michael Cadotte.*

PROM QUEEN
8" (20cm) MADC, 1992 *(see Special Dolls)*..$ 275.00
PUDDIN' 14-21" (36-53cm) cloth, vinyl, 1966-1975 .....95.00
14-18" (36-46cm) 1987 .....85.00
14-21" (36-53cm) 1990-1994 ....95.00-105.00
14" (36cm) only, 1994 ....90.00-100.00
PUMPKIN 22" (56cm) cloth/vinyl, 1967-1976 ....156.00
22" (56cm) w/rooted hair, 1976 ....185.00
PUSSY CAT 14-18" (36-46cm) cloth/vinyl, 1965-1994.......................95.00 up
Lively, 14" (36cm), 20" (51cm), 24" (61cm) head and limbs move, 1966-1969 ....125.00 up
14" (36cm) black, 1974-1979.......................................110.00
14" (36cm) black, re-introduced 1991-1994.......................85.00-105.00
14" (36cm) in trunk, trousseau, 1966, 1968.......................400.00 up
18" (46cm) made for FAO Schwarz, 1987 *(see Special Dolls)*.........125.00
20" (51cm) white, black 125.00
24" (61cm) 165.00

QUEEN 18" (46cm) hard plastic, white gown, velvet long cape trimmed w/fur, *Beaux Arts Series*, 1953.......................$1,265.00
18" (46cm) hard plastic, same gown, tiara as above but no cape, *Glamour Girl Series*, 1953 ....765.00
18" (46cm) hard plastic, white gown, short orlon cape, *Me and My Shadow Series*, 1954........................995.00
8" (20cm) hard plastic, orlon cape attached to purple robe, *Me and My Shadow Series*, 1954........................975.00 up
20" (51cm) hard plastic/vinyl arms, white brocade, *Dream Come True Series*, 1955 ....885.00
8" (20cm) velvet robe, 1955................................750.00
21" (53cm) white gown, *Fashion Parade Series*, 1957 ....900.00

This small *Sound of Music* set is from 1971-1973 and features dolls from 8in (20cm) to 12in (31cm) in size. This set is a personal favorite of mine! *Marge Meisinger Collection. Photograph by Michael Cadotte.*

QUEEN *continued*

10" (25cm) hard plastic, gold gown, blue sash, 1957................$ 380.00
10" (25cm) gold gown, panels on back of dress....................375.00
10" (25cm) white gown, blue sash, 1959-1963....................475.00
10" (25cm) in trunk, wardrobe, 1959 ....975.00 up
18" (46cm) *Elise*, white gown, red sash, 1963 ....775.00
W/vinyl head..810.00
21" (53cm) gold gown, 1958, 1961-1963............................850.00
18" (46cm) vinyl head, gold brocade gown, same as 1965 (rare) (21" [53cm] rooted hair, 1966)......................................1,000.00
21" (53cm) hard plastic/vinyl arms, gold brocade gown, 1965 ....800.00
Gold gown, 1968 ....745.00
10" (25cm) hard plastic, white gown, red sash, 1972-1973 ....365.00
14" (36cm) *Classic Dolls*, 1990......................................98.00
QUEEN ALEXANDRINE 21" (53cm) composition, 1939-1941..........1,800.00
QUEEN CHARLOTTE 10" (25cm) MADC, 1991 *(see Special Dolls)*......300.00
QUEEN ELIZABETH I 10" (25cm) made for My Doll House, 1990 *(see Special Dolls)* 200.00
QUEEN ELIZABETH II 8" (20cm) 40th anniversary, mid-year release, 1992 *(see Special Dolls)*.......................................130.00
QUEEN ISABELLA 8" (20cm) 1992 ....95.00
21" (53cm) one-of-a-kind Disney® World Auction, 1991 *(see Special Dolls)* 6,750.00

QUEEN OF HEARTS
8" (20cm) straight legs, *Storyland Dolls*, 1987-1990.............90.00
10" (25cm) Disney®, #4 Annual Showcase of Dolls, 1992 *(see Special Dolls)*........ ....475.00

QUINTUPLETS
(SO CALLED FISHER QUINTS)
hard plastic, 1964 ....700.00 set

Part of the *Portrette Series*, this *Queen* is a 10in (25cm) all hard plastic doll, made from 1972-1973. This doll is another personal favorite and getting harder to find in mint condition. *Marge Meisinger Collection. Photograph by Michael Cadotte.*

One of the great store specials is this 10in (25cm) all hard plastic *Jane Avril* made in 1989 for Marshall Fields. *Marge Meisinger Collection. Photograph by Michael Cadotte.*

QUIZ-KINS
8" (20cm) hard plastic, in
 romper,1953 ....$ 510.00
Bride, 1953-1954 ....700.00
Girl w/wig, 1953-1954 ....585.00
Groom, 1953-1954..................535.00
Peter Pan, caracul wig,
 1953 ....800.00

R

RACHEL 8" (20cm) a few tagged *Rachael*, made for
Belk & Leggett, 1989 *(see Special Dolls)*...$ 75.00
RANDOLPH, MARTHA 1st set, *First Ladies Series*, 1976-1978 ....135.00
RAPUNZEL 10" (25cm) *Portrette*, 1989-1992..115.00
RAPUNZEL & MOTHER GOTHEL 14" (36cm), 8" (20cm)
Classic Dolls, 1993-1994..250.00
REBECCA 14-17" (36-43cm), 21" (53cm) composition,
 1940-1941..600.00-1,000.00
 14" (36cm) hard plastic, 1948-1949 ....965.00
 14" (36cm) plastic/vinyl, two-tiered skirt in pink,
  Classic Dolls, 1968-1969 ....300.00
 one-piece skirt, pink dotted or checked dress, 1970-1985 ....95.00
 blue dress w/striped pinafore, 1986-1987................................60.00
RED BOY 8" (20cm) hard plastic, bend knee, 1972 ....115.00
 1973-1975, straight legs..75.00
 1976-1988, straight legs..70.00
RED CROSS NURSE 7" (18cm) composition, 1937, 1941-1943 ....295.00
 9" (23cm) composition, 1939, 1942-1943..325.00
 14" (36cm) hard plastic, 1948 ....900.00

Sears had an exclusive set of 12in (31cm) vinyl *Little Women* dolls and *Laurie* in 1989-1990. The costumes were exclusive to Sears. They are difficult to find today. *A. Glenn Mandeville Collection.*

RED RIDING HOOD
   16" (41cm) cloth/
     felt, 1930s.$ 700.00
   7" (18cm)
     composition,
     1936-1942.....320.00
   9" (23cm)
     composition,
     1939-1940.....350.00
   8" (20cm) hard
     plastic, straight leg
     walker, 1955...395.00

8" (20cm) hard plastic, bend knee walker, *Storyland Dolls*, 1962-1965 ....345.00
8" (20cm) hard plastic, bend knee, 1965-1972 ....150.00
8" (20cm) hard plastic, straight legs, 1973-1975 ....80.00
8" (20cm) hard plastic, straight legs, 1976-1986 ....72.00
8" (20cm) hard plastic, straight legs, 1987-1990 ....55.00
8" (20cm) hard plastic, straight legs, 1991-1994 ....55.00
RENOIR 21" (53cm) composition, 1945-1946 ....1,875.00
14" (36cm) hard plastic, 1950 ....900.00
21" (53cm) hard plastic/vinyl arms, 1961 ....885.00
18" (46cm) hard plastic/vinyl arms, vinyl head, 1963 ....650.00
21" (53cm) hard plastic/vinyl arms, pink gown, 1965 ....750.00
21" (53cm) blue gown w/black trim, 1966 ....1,865.00
21" (53cm) navy blue gown, red hat, 1967 ....675.00
10" (25cm) hard plastic, all navy w/red hat, 1968 ....470.00
21" (53cm) yellow gown, full lace overdress, 1969-1970 ....700.00
10" (25cm) pale blue gown, short jacket, stripe or dotted skirt, 1969 ....555.00
10" (25cm) all aqua satin, 1970 ....465.00
21" (53cm) all yellow two-piece gown pleated underskirt, 1971 ....675.00
21" (53cm) pink gown w/black jacket and trim, 1972 ....670.00
21" (53cm) hard plastic/vinyl arms, yellow gold gown,
   black ribbon, 1973 ....650.00

For the 1990 Walt Disney World® Teddy Bear and Doll Convention, this great 12in (31cm) vinyl and hard plastic *Snow White* was available for purchase by registered guests. *Marge Meisinger Collection. Photograph by Michael Cadotte.*

RENOIR CHILD
12" (31cm) plastic/ vinyl, *Portrait Children Series*, 1967...........$200.00
14" (36cm) 1968..........225.00

RENOIR GIRL
14" (36cm) plastic/ vinyl, white dress, red ribbon trim, *Portrait Children Series*, 1967-1968.......250.00

Pink dress, white pinafore, 1969-1971 ....110.00
Pink multi-tiered lace gown, 1972-1986 ....70.00
Pink pleated nylon dress, 1986..70.00

RENOIR GIRL WITH WATERING CAN *Classic Dolls and Fine Arts Series*, 1986-1987.....................75.00
W/hoop, *Classic Dolls* and *Fine Arts Series*, 1986-1987...........75.00

RHETT
12" (31cm) plastic/vinyl, *Portrait Children Series*, 1981-1985...............................85.00
8" (20cm) hard plastic, *Jubilee II*, 1989.......................95.00
8" (20cm) hard plastic, *Scarlett Series*, 1991-1994...................60.00

RIDING HABIT 8" (20cm) *Americana Series*, 1990.............90.00

RILEY'S LITTLE ANNIE
14" (36cm) plastic/vinyl, *Literature Series*, 1967.................200.00

RINGBEARER 14" (36cm) hard plastic, 1951.............................540.00

RING MASTER 8" (20cm) hard plastic, CU Gathering, 1991 *(see Special Dolls)*...................180.00

For 1991, A Child at Heart featured this 8in (20cm) *Easter bunny* with a selection of hair colors. *Marge Meisinger Collection. Photograph by Michael Cadotte.*

106

In 1992, an 8in (20cm) and a 14in (36cm) doll were combined to make this *Rumplestiltskin* and the *Miller's Daughter* set come alive. Set is complete with the spinning wheel! *Marge Meisinger Collection. Photograph by Michael Cadotte.*

RIVERBOAT QUEEN - LENA 8" (20cm) hard plastic, MADC, 1990
(see Special Dolls) ....$ 385.00
ROBIN HOOD 8" (20m) *Storyland Dolls*, 1988-1990.............................85.00
RODEO 8" (20cm) hard plastic, 1955 ....975.00

ROLLER SKATING
8" (20cm) hard plastic,
1953-1955 ....550.00
ROMANCE 21" (53cm)
composition, 1945-1946 ...1,565.00
ROMEO 18" (46cm)
composition, 1949......1,250.00
8" (20cm) hard plastic,
1955 ....990.00 up
8" (20cm) hard plastic,
Storyland Collection, mid-year
release, 1994 ....95.00

My Little Sweetheart was a 1992 store exclusive for A Child at Heart. The heart shaped candy box with Madame Alexander's signature came with the doll. This 8in (20cm) all hard plastic doll was offered in a variety of hair colors and in a black version as well. *Marge Meisinger Collection. Photograph by Michael Cadotte.*

ROMEO continued
   12" (31cm) plastic/
      vinyl, *Portrait*
      Children Series,
      1978-1987.....$ 80.00
   12" (31cm) re-introduced,
      Romance Series,
      1991-1992 ....92.00
ROOSEVELT, EDITH
   5th set, *First Ladies*
      Series, 1988............85.00
ROOSEVELT, ELEANOR
   14" (36cm) plastic,
      vinyl, 6th set, *First*
      Ladies Series,
      1989-1990 ....100.00
ROSAMUND BRIDESMAID   15"
   (38cm) hard plastic, 1951 ....525.00
   18" (46cm) hard plastic, 1951 ....600.00
ROSE   9" (23cm) early vinyl toddler, pink organdy dress and bonnet, 1953 ..125.00
ROSEBUD   16-19" (41-48cm)
   cloth/vinyl, 1952-1953.....165.00
   13" (33cm) 1953...............185.00
   23-25" (58-64cm) 1953....200.00
   14-20" (36-51cm)
      white, 1986......................60.00
   14" (36cm) black................80.00
ROSE FAIRY
   8" (20cm) hard plastic,
      1956.......................1,250.00 up

Happy Birthday, 1992-1994 and *Happy Birthday Billy*, 1993-1994, are wonderful 8in (20cm) dolls. Like others in the line, they were available in assorted hair colors and in an African-American version as well. *A. Glenn Mandeville Collection.*

Faith is an 8in (20cm) hard plastic doll made for the 1992 Collector's United Gathering in Atlanta, Georgia. She came with her accessories in a hat box. *Marge Meisinger Collection. Photograph by Michael Cadotte.*

ROSETTE 10" (25cm)
Portrette Series,
1987-1989..............$ 75.00
ROSEY POSEY
14" (36cm) cloth/vinyl,
1976..........................80.00
21" (53cm) cloth/vinyl,
1976......................110.00
ROSS, BETSY
8" (20cm) hard plastic, bend knee, *Americana Series,*
1967-1972 ....160.00
1976 Bicentennial gown w/star print...............................140.00
Straight legs, *Storyland Dolls,* 1973-1975........................70.00
Straight legs, 1976-1987 ....70.00
8" (20cm) re-introduced, *Americana Series,* 1991-1992.................55.00
ROSY
14" (36cm) 1988-1990...75.00
ROUND UP DAY MOUSEKETEER 8" (20cm) made for Disney®,
1992 *(see Special Dolls)* 80.00
ROXANNE 8" (20cm) hard plastic, *Storyland Dolls,* 1994...................60.00
ROYAL WEDDING 21" (53cm) composition, 1939...................1,600.00 up
ROZY 12" (31cm) plastic/vinyl, 1969 ....485.00
RUBY (JULY) 10" (25cm) hard plastic, *Birthstone Collection,* 1992..........80.00
RUFFLES CLOWN 21" (53cm) 1954 ....435.00
RUMANIA 8" (20cm) hard plastic, bend knee, 1968-1972 ....145.00
8" (20cm) straight legs, 1973-1975 ....78.00
8" (20cm) straight legs, 1976-1987 ....72.00
8" (20cm) white face, 1986...55.00
RUMBERA, RUMBERO 7" (18cm) composition, 1938-1943................250.00 each
9" (23cm) composition, 1939-1941 ....325.00 each
RUMPELSTILTSKIN & MILLER'S DAUGHTER 8" (20cm) and
14" (36cm) limited to 3,000 sets, 1992 ....250.00
RUSSIA 8" (20cm) hard plastic, bend knee, 1968-1972 ....147.00
8" (20cm) straight legs, 1973-1975 ....75.00
8" (20cm) straight legs, 1976-1988 ....55.00
8" (20cm) white face, 1985-1987 ....55.00
8" (20cm) re-introduced 1991-1992 ....52.00
8" (20cm) hard plastic, *International Series,* 1994.................50.00
RUSSIAN 7" (18cm) composition, 1935-1938..............................285.00
RUSTY 20" (51cm) cloth/vinyl, 1967-1968 ....375.00

This 8in (20cm) hard plastic *Queen Elizabeth II* was the 1992 Alexander Doll Company mid-year release. *A. Glenn Mandeville Collection.*

SAILOR
14" (36cm) composition, ...$ 800.00
17" (43cm) composition, 1943-1944.......................................950.00
8" (20cm) boy, UFDC, 1990 *(see Special Dolls)*.....................700.00
8" (20cm) hard plastic, boy, made for FAO Schwarz, 1991
   (see Special Dolls) 80.00
12" (31cm) hard plastic, *Classic Lissy,* see Columbian Sailor,
   UFDC, 1993 *(see Special Dolls)*......................................350.00
SAILORETTE 10" (25cm) hard plastic, *Portrette Series,* 1988 ....75.00
SAKS OWN CHRISTMAS CAROL 8" (20cm) hard plastic, made for
  Saks Fifth Avenue, 1993 *(see Special Dolls)* 70.00
SALLY BRIDE 14" (36cm) composition, 1938-1939................................450.00
18-21" (46-53cm) composition, 1938-1939...............525.00-700.00

SALOME
14" (36cm) *Opera Series,*
1984-1986...................90.00

SAMANTHA
14" (36cm) made for
FAO Schwarz,
1989 *(see Special
Dolls)*.....................170.00
14" (36cm) gold
ruffled gown,
Classic Dolls,
1991-1992...............170.00

This great looking doll is *Mardi Gras,* a 10in (25cm) all hard plastic doll made for Spiegel in 1992. *Marge Meisinger Collection. Photograph by Michael Cadotte.*

Halloween is definitely here with this 8in (20cm) hard plastic set of *Trick and Treat* from A Child at Heart in 1993. The stand, by Ann Rast, was offered for purchase with the dolls. *Marge Meisinger Collection. Photograph by Michael Cadotte.*

SANDY MCHARE cloth/felt, 1930s......................$ 700.00
SANTA CLAUS
8" (20cm) mid-year release, 1993.................65.00
SAPPHIRE (SEPTEMBER)
10" (25cm) hard plastic, *Birthstone Collection,* 1992.............................64.00
SARDINIA 8" (20cm) hard plastic, 1989-1991........55.00
SARGENT 14" (36cm) plastic/vinyl, dressed in lavender, *Fine Arts Series*, 1984-1985.........75.00
SARGENT'S GIRL
14" (36cm) plastic/vinyl, dressed in pink *Fine Arts Series*, 1986.......75.00
SCARECROW 8" (20cm) hard plastic, *Wizard of Oz Series*, 1993-1994...60.00
SCARLETT O'HARA (pre-movie, 1937-1938)
7" (18cm) composition, 1937-1939 ....500.00 up

11" (28cm) composition, 1940-1943 ....650.00
9" (23cm) composition, 1938-1941 ....500.00
18" (46cm) composition, 1939-1946 ....800.00
14-15" (36-38cm) composition, 1941-1943........800.00 up
21" (53cm) composition, 1942-1946 ....1,400.00 up
8" (20cm) hard plastic, yellow, blue, pink, 1955........................1,400.00 up
8" (20cm) hard plastic, straight leg walker, pink, yellow or blue floral gown, 1956........................1,400.00 up

Jack Be Nimble was an event exclusive for Dolly Dears in 1993. He is a factory altered doll and is 8in (20cm) tall in hard plastic. *Marge Meisinger Collection. Photograph by Michael Cadotte.*

Caroline's Storyland Trunk was a 1993 Neiman Marcus store special, that contained an 8in (20cm) hard plastic doll with lots of fairy tale costumes. *Marge Meisinger Collection. Photograph by Michael Cadotte.*

SCARLETT O'HARA *continued*

8" (20cm) hard plastic, bend knee walker, white, lace and red ribbon trim, 1957 (extremely rare) ....$1,400.00 up

20" (51cm) jointed arms, *Cissy, Scarlett* w/deep green velvet gown, matching jacket and bonnet trimmed in light green net, 1958 (rare).....................................2,600.00 up

21" (53cm) *Cissy, Scarlett* w/straight arms, gown of white organdy trimmed w/lace beading apple green inserted ribbons on tiers of skirt, white horsehair braid picture hat, 1961 (rare) ....2,500.00 up

21" (53cm) *Cissy, Scarlett* straight arms, blue taffeta gown w/black braid trim w/matching coat and bonnet, 1961..1,700.00 up

12" (31cm) hard plastic, green taffeta gown and bonnet, 1963 (rare)..1,300.00

18" (46cm) hard plastic/vinyl arms, pale blue organdy w/rosebuds and straw hat, 1963 only ....700.00 up

8" (20cm) hard plastic, bend knee, in white or cream gown, 1965 ....750.00 up

21" (53cm) hard plastic/vinyl arms, green taffeta gown, 1965 ....1,800.00 up

8" (20cm) hard plastic, bend knee, flowered gown, *Americana Series* and *Storyland Dolls*, 1966-1972 ....375.00 up

21" (53cm) plastic/vinyl, all white gown, red sash and roses variations, 1966 (referred to as Coco) ....2,700.00 up

21" (53cm) plastic/vinyl, green taffeta gown w/black trim, 1967 ....650.00 up

10" (25cm) hard plastic, lace in bonnet, green taffeta gown w/black braid trim, 1968...475.00 up

14" (36cm) plastic/vinyl, floral gown, 1968.......................800.00

14" (36cm) plastic/vinyl, white gown w/rows of lace, 1968-1986..........................125.00

21" (53cm) plastic/vinyl, floral print gown w/wide white hem, 1968..............................1,000.00

10" (25cm) hard plastic, green taffeta gown w/white and gold braid trim, 1969.......450.00 up

This *Scarlett O'Hara* is a recreation of a doll produced by the Alexander Doll Company in the late 1930s. She is 8in (20cm) tall and was a 1993 mid-year release. *A. Glenn Mandeville Collection.*

The gorgeous 10in (25cm) hard plastic *Snow White* was a Walt Disney World®/Disneyland® special in 1993. *A. Glenn Mandeville Collection.*

SCARLETT O'HARA *continued*

21" (53cm) plastic/vinyl, green taffeta white braid trim, 1969..........$ 700.00

10" (25cm) hard plastic, green taffeta gown w/gold braid trim, 1970-1973...............450.00

21" (53cm) plastic/vinyl, green taffeta, white trim on jacket, 1970....725.00 up

8" (20cm) hard plastic, bright pink floral trim, 1971 only...........450.00 up

8" (20cm) hard plastic, in white gown, 1973-1985 ....75.00

21" (53cm) plastic/vinyl, all green taffeta, white lace at cuffs, 1975-1977 ....450.00 up

21" (53cm) plastic/vinyl, silk floral gown, green parasol, white lace, 1978 ....400.00 up

21" (53cm) plastic/vinyl, green velvet, 1979-1985 ....375.00

12" (31cm) plastic/vinyl, green gown w/braid trim, 1981-1985 ....95.00

8" (20cm) hard plastic, white gown w/red sash, MADC, 1986 *(see Special Dolls)* 350.00

14" (36cm) plastic/vinyl, *Jubilee I*, all green velvet, 1986................200.00

21" (53cm) plastic/vinyl, floral gown, green parasol, 1986...............................450.00

8" (20cm) hard plastic, white face, blue dot gown, 1987 (rare)...............................225.00 up

21" (53cm) plastic/vinyl, layered all over white gown, 1987-1988 ....400.00

14" (36cm) plastic/vinyl, blue floral print, 1987-1989...175.00

8" (20cm) hard plastic, straight legs, flowered gown, 1986-1989 ....75.00

8" (20cm) hard plastic, *Jubilee II*, all green velvet gown, 1989...............................145.00 up

In 1993, the Madame Alexander Doll Club offered its members this lovely 8in (20cm) doll, called *Wendy Loves Being Best Friends*. *A. Glenn Mandeville Collection.*

Believed to be one of the first *Scarlett* dolls issued, this late 1930s all composition *Scarlett O'Hara* has a human hair wig and is 11in (28cm) tall. Her costume was duplicated for the 1993 mid-year release. *A. Glenn Mandeville Collection.*

SCARLETT *continued*

10" (25cm) hard plastic, *Jubliee II*, burgundy and white gown, 1989...$ 150.00

14" (36cm) plastic/vinyl, *Jubilee II,* green floral print gown, 1989 ....150.00

21" (53cm) plastic/vinyl, red gown, (birthday party dress) 1989 ....400.00

8" (20cm) hard plastic, MADC,1990 *(see Special Dolls)*..185.00

8" (20cm) hard plastic, straight legs, tiny floral print, *Scarlett Series*, 1990..75.00

14" (36cm) plastic/vinyl, tiny floral print gown, *Scarlett Series*, 1990 ....135.00 up

10" (25cm) hard plastic, floral print gown, *Scarlett Series*, 1990-1991 .....95.00

21" (53cm) plastic/vinyl, Bride, *Scarlett Series*, 1990-1993 ....375.00

8" (20cm) hard plastic, four-tier white gown, curly hair, 1991 only......75.00

21" (53cm) porcelain, green velvet, gold trim, 1991 ....650.00

14" (36cm) plastic/vinyl, white ruffles, green ribbon, *Scarlett Series*, 1991-1992..175.00

21" (53cm) plastic/vinyl, green on white, three ruffles around skirt, 1991-1992 ....325.00

8" (20cm) hard plastic, rose floral print, oversized bonnet, 1992..........................75.00

10" (25cm) hard plastic, *Scarlett at the Ball*, all in black, 1992.........................150.00

8" (20cm) hard plastic, green and white stripe gown, 1993...........................75.00

A 16in (41cm) all porcelain *Annette Funicello* doll was a real surprise in 1993. Sculpted by Robert Tonner for the Alexander Doll Company, the doll was designed for a function at Walt Disney World® to honor Annette. The left over dolls were eagerly snapped up when sold at the Park, after the event. Lucky indeed is the collector who has this very limited doll. *A. Glenn Mandeville Collection.*

In 1993, the Alexander Doll Company honored Madame Alexander with this 8in (20cm) *Wendy Honors Madame.* The doll featured a dress that the 21in (53cm) *Portrait* doll of Madame Alexander wore. *A. Glenn Mandeville Collection.*

SCARLETT O'HARA *continued*
8" (20cm) hard plastic, in trunk, *Honeymoon in New Orleans,* 1993-1994.........................$ 200.00
8" (20cm) hard plastic, 70th Anniversary, mid-year release, 1993.....................................125.00
10" (25cm) hard plastic, green velvet w/gold trim, 1993-1994............................100.00
10" (25cm) hard plastic, red dress and boa, 1994.......................100.00
8" (20cm) hard plastic, Bride, 1994......................................70.00
8" (20cm) hard plastic, picnic, 1994......................................65.00
21" (53cm) plastic/vinyl, *Portrait, Scarlett Series,* 1994 ....300.00

SCHOOL GIRL 7" (18cm) composition, 1936-1943............................300.00

SCOTCH 7" (18cm) composition, 1936-1939...................................285.00
9" (23cm) composition, 1939-1940 ....310.00
10" (25cm) hard plastic, 1962-1963.....................................765.00 up

SCOTLAND BOY 8" (20cm) hard plastic, *International Series,* 1994 .....50.00

SCOTS LASS 8" (20cm) hard plastic, bend knee walker, 1963............265.00

SCOTTISH (SCOTLAND) 8" (20cm) hard plastic, bend knee walker, 1964-1965 ....250.00
8" (20cm) hard plastic, bend knee, 1965-1972 ....165.00
8" (20cm) straight legs, 1973-1975..90.00

8" (20cm) straight legs, 1976-1993 ....52.00

SCOUTING 8" (20cm) hard plastic, *Americana Series,* 1991-1992..55.00

SEPTEMBER 14" (36cm) plastic/vinyl, *Classic Dolls,* 1989..75.00

SEVEN DWARFS 9" (23cm) composition, 1937....................500.00 each

America's Junior Miss is a stunning 8in (20cm) hard plastic doll that was a special for Dian and Gary Green's newspaper, *Collectors United,* in 1994. She was available in a variety of hair colors. *Marge Meisinger Collection. Photograph by Michael Cadotte.*

This 8in (20cm) doll is *Maypole Dance* and was a 1994 exclusive for Shirley's Doll House. *A. Glenn Mandeville Collection.*

SHAHARAZAD
10" (25cm) hard plastic, *Portrette Series*, 1992-1993...............$ 84.00
SHEA 8" (20cm) hard plastic, elf, CU Gathering, 1990 *(see Special Dolls)* 200.00
SICILY 8" (20cm) hard plastic, 1989-1990 ....75.00
SIMONE 21" (53cm) hard plastic/ vinyl arms, in trunk, 1968 (same doll as *Jacqueline*)...1,900.00
SIR LAPIN HARE cloth/felt, 1930s 675.00
SISTER BRENDA 8" (20cm) hard plastic, made for FAO Schwarz, *(see Special Dolls)* 275.00
SITTING PRETTY 18" (46cm) cloth body, 1965 (rare) 425.00
SKATER 15-18" (38-46cm) hard plastic/vinyl, 1955-1956........................650.00
SLEEPING BEAUTY 7-9" (18-23cm) composition, 1941-1944 ....360.00
15-16" (38-41cm) composition 1938-1940..................450.00
18-21" (46-53cm) composition, 1941-1944..................600.00
16-1/2" (42cm) hard plastic, 1959...........................575.00
21" (53cm) hard plastic, 1959...........................915.00
10" (25cm) hard plastic, 1959-1960..................475.00
14" (36cm) plastic/vinyl, gold gown, *Classic Dolls*, 1971-1985..................100.00
14" (36cm) plastic/vinyl, blue gown, *Classic Dolls*, 1986-1990..................125.00
10" (25cm) hard plastic, *Portrette Series*, 1991-1992....................95.00
21" (53cm) plastic/vinyl, Disney® World Auction, 1989 *(see Special Dolls)*......................2,950.00

Who could resist this 8in (20cm) pair of Tweedledee & Tweedledum, made for purchase by registered guests of the 1994 Walt Disney World® Teddy Bear and Doll Convention. *A. Glenn Mandeville Collection.*

A serene and knowing face graces this 8in (20cm) *Navajo Woman* that was the souvenir doll for the 1994 Madame Alexander Doll Club Convention. *A. Glenn Mandeville Collection.*

SLUMBERMATE
12" (31cm) cloth/
  composition,
  1940s......................$ 200.00
13" (33cm) vinyl/
  cloth, 1951................155.00
21" (53cm) composition/
  cloth, 1940s...............300.00

SMARTY
12" (31cm) plastic/vinyl,
  1962-1963.................300.00
Smarty & Baby, 1963 (rare) 350.00
W/boy "Artie" in case w/wardrobe, 1963 (very rare) ....1,000.00 up
SMEE 8" (20cm) Storyland Dolls, 1993-1994 ....55.00
SMILEY 20" (51cm) cloth/vinyl, 1971 ....285.00
SMOKEY TAIL cloth/felt, 1930s 700.00
SNOW FLAKE 10" (25cm) hard
plastic, *Portrette Series*, 1993...85.00
SNOW QUEEN 10" (25cm) hard plastic,
Portrette Series, 1991-1992 ....84.00
SNOW WHITE 12" (31cm) composition, 1939-1940 ....425.00
13" (33cm) composition, painted
  eyes, 1937-1939...450.00
13" (33cm) composition, sleep eyes,
  1939-1940...400.00
16" (41cm) composition,

1939-1942 ....500.00
18" (46cm) composition,
  1939-1940 ....670.00
15" (38cm), 18" (46cm),
  23" (58cm) hard plastic,
  1952 ....675.00, 850.00, 995.00
14" (36cm) plastic/vinyl,
  white gown,
  Classic Dolls, 1968-1985 ....175.00
  Ecru and gold gown, red cape,
    1986-1992 ....120.00
14" (36cm) plastic/vinyl, Disney®
  license, 1967-1977 ....425.00

The Doll and Teddy Bear Expo, sponsored by Collector Communications and held in Arlington, VA in 1994, had exclusive dolls available for purchase. This is an 8in (20cm) *Shadow of the Madame*, available to attendees at the event. *A. Glenn Mandeville Collection.*

Collectors were caught off guard when the Disney Catalog featured this exclusive 14in (36cm) vinyl *Sleeping Beauty*. Announced in 1994, the doll was not shipped until 1995. She is dressed in her Briar Rose outfit and comes with her blue ballgown and accessories. The wrist tag featured the same lettering style as the 1959 dolls. *A. Glenn Mandeville Collection.*

SNOW WHITE *continued*
    8" (20cm) hard plastic, Disney® Colors, 1972-1976 *(see Special Dolls)* ....$ 450.00
    12" (31cm) plastic/ vinyl, made for Disney® 1990 *(see Special Dolls)* 200.00
  8" (20cm) *Storyland Dolls*, 1990-1992 ....55.00
  10" (25cm) Disneyland/Disney® World, 1993 *(see Special Dolls)* ..150.00
SO BIG 22" (56cm) cloth/vinyl, painted eyes, 1968-1975................270.00
SO LITE BABY OR TODDLER 20" (51cm) cloth, 1930s.......................500.00 up
SOLDIER 14" (36cm) composition, 1943-1944.................................775.00 up
  17" (43cm) composition, 1942-1945...875.00 up
SOUND OF MUSIC All in same outfit: red skirt, white attached blouse,
    black vest that ties in front w/gold thread,
    ca. 1965 (very rare)..400.00-550.00 up each
SOUND OF MUSIC, DRESSED IN SAILOR SUITS & TAGGED, CA. 1965
  10" (25cm) Friedrich..365.00
  10" (25cm) Gretl 365.00
  10" (25cm) Marta...365.00
  14" (36cm) Louisa 500.00
  14" (36cm) Brigitta 400.00
  14" (36cm) Liesl..400.00
  17" (43cm) Maria...500.00
  Set of 7 dolls ....N/A
SOUND OF MUSIC, LARGE SET, 1965-1970
  10" (25cm) Friedrich..225.00
  10" (25cm) Marta, 10" (25cm) Gretl ....225.00 each
  14" (36cm) Brigitta, 14" (36cm) Liesl ....225.00 each
  14" (36cm) Louisa 350.00
  17" (43cm) Maria...395.00
  Full set of 7 dolls 1,900.00
SOUND OF MUSIC, SMALL SET, 1971-1973
  8" (20cm) Marta, 8" (20cm) Friedrich, 8" (20cm) Gretl ....175.00 each
  10" (25cm) Brigitta..250.00
  10" (25cm) Liesl..250.00
  10" (25cm) Louisa...295.00 up

SOUND OF MUSIC, SMALL SET, 1971-1973 *continued*
 12" (31cm) Maria ....$ 350.00
 Set of 7 dolls ....1,700.00 up
SOUND OF MUSIC, RE-INTRODUCED 1992-1993
 8" (20cm) Brigitta..55.00
 8" (20cm) Gretl and Kurt (boy in sailor suit)................................62.00 each
 10" (25cm) Maria..85.00
 12" (31cm) Maria Bride...132.00
SOUND OF MUSIC 1993 (continuation of set)
 8" (20cm) Friedrich...55.00
 8" (20cm) Marta...55.00
 10" (25cm) Liesl 75.00
 10" (25cm) Maria at the Abby 70.00
SOUTH AMERICAN 7" (18cm) composition, 1938-1943 ....315.00
 9" (23cm) composition, 1939-1941 ....335.00
SOUTHERN BELLE OR GIRL 8" (20cm) hard plastic, 1953-1954.......985.00 up
 8" (20cm) hard plastic, 1955 ....800.00
 8" (20cm) hard plastic, 1956 ....950.00
 8" (20cm) hard plastic, 1963...475.00
 12" (31cm) hard plastic, 1963...1,235.00
 21" (53cm) hard plastic/vinyl arms,
   blue gown w/wide pleated hem, 1965...975.00
   White gown w/green ribbon trim, 1967 ....700.00
 10" (25cm) hard plastic, white gown w/green ribbon thru three
   rows of lace, 1968...450.00
 10" (25cm) white gown w/rows of lace, pink sash, 1969 ....450.00
 10" (25cm) hard plastic, white gown w/red ribbon sash, 1970.................450.00
 10" (25cm) hard plastic, white gown w/green ribbon sash,
   1971-1973 ....440.00
 10" (25cm) made for My Doll House, 1989 *(see Special Dolls)*...150.00
SOUTHERN GIRL 11-14" (28-36cm) composition, 1940-1943 ....500.00
 17-21" (43-53cm) composition, 1940-1943 ....700.00-800.00
SPAIN 8" (20cm) hard plastic, *International Series*, 1994 ....60.00
SPANISH 7-8" (18-20cm) composition, 1935-1939 ....290.00
 9" (23cm) composition, 1936-1940 ....315.00
SPANISH BOY 8" (20cm) hard plastic, bend knee and bend knee
   walker, 1964-1968..375.00
SPANISH GIRL 8" (20cm) hard plastic, bend knee walker,
   three-tiered skirt, 1962-1965 ....200.00
 8" (20cm) hard plastic, bend knee, three-tiered skirt, 1965-1972..165.00
 8" (20cm) straight legs, three-tiered skirt, 1973-1975.....................120.00
 8" (20cm) straight legs, three-tiered skirt, 1976-1982.....................110.00
 8" (20cm) straight legs, two-tiered skirt, 1983-1985........................55.00
 8" (20cm) straight legs, white w/red polka dots, 1986-1989 ....60.00
 8" (20cm) straight legs, all red tiered skirt, 1990-1992....................55.00

SPANISH MATADOR 8" (20cm) 1992-1993...$ 55.00
SPECIAL GIRL 23-24" (58-61cm) cloth/composition, 1942-1946........485.00
SPRING 14" (36cm) plastic/vinyl, *Classic Dolls*, 1993.......................150.00
SPRING BREAK 8" (20cm) hard plastic, Metroplex Doll Club,
   1992 *(see Special Dolls)*...350.00
SPRING FLOWERS 14" (36cm) plastic/vinyl, *Classic Dolls*, 1994 ....120.00
SPRINGTIME 8" (20cm) MADC, 1991 *(see Special Dolls)*.................200.00
STILTS 8" (20cm) hard plastic clown on suits, 1992-1993...................60.00
STORY PRINCESS 8" (20cm) hard plastic/vinyl, 1956 ....1,250.00
   15", 18" (38cm, 46cm) hard plastic/vinyl, costume change, 1956...800.00 up
   15-18" (38-46cm) hard plastic, 1954 ....700.00 up
   15" (38cm) hard plastic/vinyl, costume change, 1955 ....700.00 up
STUFFY *(see Little Men)*
SUELLEN 14-17" (36-43cm) composition, 1937-1938.....................995.00
   12" (31cm) yellow, multi-tiered skirt, *Scarlett Series*, 1990...............75.00
   12" (31cm) made for Jean's Dolls, 1992 *(see Special Dolls)* 165.00
   8" (20cm) hard plastic, *Scarlett Series*, 1994.................................55.00

The Belk & Leggett store specials are always a collector favorite. This is *Holly*, an 8in (20cm) all hard plastic doll made in 1994. *Photograph Courtesy of Scott-Lancaster.*

SUGAR DARLIN'
14-18" (36-46cm)
cloth/vinyl,
1964................$ 150.00
14" (36cm), 18" (46cm),
24" (61cm) *Lively*,
knob makes head
and limbs move,
1964........150.00-190.00
24" (61cm) 1964....200.00
SUGAR PLUM FAIRY
10" (25cm) *Portrette Series*, 1992-1993....92.00
SUGAR TEARS
12" (31cm) vinyl baby,
1964........................125.00
SULKY SUE 8" (20cm)
1988-1990................90.00

SUMMER 14" (36cm) *Classic Dolls*, 1993 ....135.00
SUMMER SKIES 14" (36cm) *Classic Dolls*, 1994 ....125.00
SUNBONNET SUE 9" (23cm) composition, 1937-1940 ....350.00
SUNFLOWER CLOWN 40" (101cm) all cloth, flower eyes, 1951................825.00
SUSANNA 8" (20cm) made for Dolly Dears, 1992 *(see Special Dolls)*............250.00
SUSIE Q cloth, 1940-1942 ....675.00
SUZY 12" (31cm) plastic/vinyl, 1970...365.00
SWEDEN (SWISS)
8" (20cm) hard plastic, bend knee walker, 1961-1965 ....195.00
8" (20cm) bend knee walker w/smile face, 1963.................................225.00
8" (20cm) hard plastic, bend knee, 1965-1972 ....150.00
8" (20cm) straight legs, 1973-1975... 75.00
8" (20cm) straight legs, 1976-1989..55.00
8" (20cm) white face, 1986 ....55.00
8" (20cm) re-introduced 1991 only 55.00
SWEDISH
7" (18cm) composition, 1936-1940...290.00
9" (23cm) composition, 1937-1941...315.00
8" (20cm) hard plastic, bend knee, 1965-1969, 1972-1973 ....150.00
SWEET BABY
18-1/2-20" (47-51cm) cloth/latex, 1948 ....55.00-70.00
14" (36cm) 1983-1984 ....65.00
14" (36cm) 1987-1993 ....75.00
14" (36cm) in carry case, 1990-1992 ....95.00-125.00
SWEET SIXTEEN 14" (36cm) *Classic Dolls*, 1991-1992 ....120.00

Neiman Marcus presented this *Caroline Travels the World* as a store exclusive in 1994. She is an 8in (20cm) all hard plastic doll and features several authentic ethnic costumes. *Marge Meisinger Collection. Photograph by Michael Cadotte.*

SWEET TEARS 9" (23cm) vinyl, 1965-1974 ....$ 65.00
    14" (36cm) in window box, 1965-1974..155.00 up
    9" (23cm) vinyl, w/layette in box, discontinued 1973 ....175.00
    14" (36cm) 1965-1982...55.00
    16" (41cm) 1965-1971..95.00
    14" (36cm) in trunk, trousseau, 1967-1974 ....245.00 up
    14" (36cm) w/layette, 1979..170.00
SWEET VIOLET   18" (46cm) hard plastic, jointed, 1954 only ....800.00 up
SWEETIE BABY   22" (56cm) all plastic, 1962 ....170.00
SWEETIE WALKER   23" (58cm) all plastic, 1962.................................295.00
SWISS   7" (18cm) composition, 1936...350.00
    9" (23cm) composition, 1935-1938 ....365.00
    10" (25cm) hard plastic, 1962-1963 ....950.00
    8" (20cm) hard plastic, bend knee walker, smile face, 1963...............250.00
    8" (20cm) hard plastic, bend knee, 1968-1972...................................155.00
SWITZERLAND   8" (20cm) hard plastic, bend knee walker, 1961-1965 ......245.00
    8" (20cm) hard plastic, bend knee, 1965-1972....................................155.00
    8" (20cm) hard plastic, straight legs, 1973-1975..................................60.00
    8" (20cm) hard plastic, straight legs, 1976-1989..................................55.00
    8" (20cm) white face, 1986..55.00

The Alexander Doll Company branched out into some other markets in 1994. Here is *Julie,* an 18in (46cm) all vinyl doll designed by Candy Spelling and marketed under the name Fantasy Dolls. *A. Glenn Mandeville Collection.*

SYLVESTER THE JESTER
14" (36cm)
plastic/vinyl,
1992-1993....$105.00

TAFT, HELEN
5th set, *First Ladies Series*, 1988....$ 85.00

TEENY TWINKLE
cloth, flirty eyes,
1946.................600.00

TEXAS 8" (20cm)
Americana Series,
1991...................60.00

TEXAS SHRINER
8" (20cm) hard plastic,
Shriner's National
Convention, 1993 *(see
Special Dolls)*...395.00

THAILAND
8" (20cm) hard
plastic, bend knee,
1966-1972......170.00
8" (20cm) straight legs, 1973-1975..70.00
8" (20cm) straight legs, 1976-1989..55.00

THOMAS, MARLO 17" (43cm) plastic/vinyl, 1967 (two versions) 650.00

THOROUGHLY MODERN WENDY 8" (20cm) made for Disney World®
Auction, 1992 *(see Special Dolls)*...85.00

THREE LITTLE PIGS 12" (31cm) composition, 1938-1939 ....700.00 each

THUMBELINA & HER LADY 8" (20cm) hard plastic and 21" (53cm)
porcelain, limited edition of 2,500 sets, 1992 ....550.00

TIBET 8" (20cm) *International Dolls*, 1993 ....50.00

TIGER LILY 8" (20cm) 1992-1993 ....55.00

TIMMY TODDLER 23" (58cm) plastic/vinyl, 1960-1961 ....175.00
30" (76cm) 1960..225.00

TIN WOODSMAN 8" (20cm) *Wizard of Oz Series*, 1993-1994.............55.00

TINKERBELL 10" (25cm) hard plastic, 1969 (and possibly later)......485.00
8" (20cm) hard plastic, Disney® Exclusive, 1973 *(see Special Dolls)* ....985.00 up
8" (20cm) hard plastic, magic wand, *Storyland Dolls*, 1991-1994.....65.00

TINY BETTY 7" (18cm) composition, 1935-1942 ....320.00

Lady and Lord Valentine were introduced in 1994 and are 8in (20cm) dolls that make St.Valentine's Day a regal holiday! *A. Glenn Mandeville Collection.*

TINY TIM
  cloth, early 1930s....$ 700.00
  7" (18cm) composition,
    1934-1937................385.00
  14" (36cm) composition,
    1938-1940................600.00
TIPPI   8" (20cm) hard plastic,
  CU Gathering, 1988
  (see Special Dolls)......375.00
TIPPY TOE   16" (41cm)
  cloth, 1940s................635.00
TOM SAWYER   8" (20cm)
  hard plastic, *Storyland
  Dolls*, 1989-1990...........60.00
TOMMY   12" (31cm) hard
  plastic, made for FAO
  Schwarz 100th Anniversary,
  1962.......................1,300.00
TOMMY BANGS
  (see Little Men)
TOMMY SNOOKS   8" (20cm)
  hard plastic, *Storyland Dolls*,
  1988-1991.....................55.00
TOMMY TITTLEMOUSE
  8" (20cm) hard plastic, *Storyland Dolls*, 1988-1991...........................55.00
TONY SARG MARIONETTES   12-14" (31-36cm) composition,
  1934-1940 ....175.00 up
TOOTH FAIRY   10" (25cm) *Portrette*, 1994 ....80.00
TOPSY-TURVY   7-9" (18-23cm) composition w/*Tiny Betty* heads, 1935..195.00
  7" (18cm) w/*Dionne Quint* head, 1936 ....365.00
TOULOUSE-LAUTREC   21" (53cm) plastic/vinyl, black and pink,
  1986-1987 ....195.00
TOY SOLDIER   8' (20cm) hard plastic, *Storyland Dolls*, 1993-1994.............55.00
TRAPEZE ARTIST
  10" (25cm) hard plastic, *Portrette Series*, 1990-1991 ....95.00
TREE TOPPER   8" (20cm) hard plastic, dolls in cones w/o legs
  Merry Angel, made for Spiegel, 1991 *(see Special Dolls)* 145.00
  Joy Noel, made for Spiegel, 1992 *(see Special Doll)*..........................105.00
  Cream, 1992..85.00
  Red, 1992...105.00
  Angel Lace, 1993 ....75.00
  Pink Victorian, 1993-1994 ....75.00
  Red Velvet, 1993..90.00
  Red, Gold & Green, 1994 ....85.00
  Ivory Lace, 1994...65.00
  White Antique, 1994 ....75.00
TREENA BALLERINA   15" (38cm) hard plastic, 1952 ....775.00

Always known for quality, Saks Fifth Avenue offered for sale, holiday 1994, this treasure of an 8in (20cm) doll entitled *Joy, The Joy of Christmas*, 1994. *A. Glenn Mandeville Collection.*

TREENA BALLERINA *continued*
  18-21" (46-53cm) 1952.....$ 955.00
TRICK AND TREAT 8" (20cm) hard plastic, made for A Child at Heart, 1993 *(see Special Dolls)*....................145.00
TRUMAN, BESS 14" (36cm) plastic/vinyl, 6th set, *First Ladies Series*, 1989-1990..................100.00
TUNSIA 8" (20cm) hard plastic, 1989..75.00
TURKEY 8" (20cm) hard plastic, bend knee, 1968-1972........145.00
  8" (20cm) straight legs, 1973-1975............................80.00
  8" (20cm) straight legs, 1976-1986............................55.00
TWEEDLEDEE & TWEEDLEDUM
  14" (36cm) cloth, 1930-1931...800.00 each
20's TRAVELER 10" (25cm) hard plastic, *Portrette Series*, 1992 only....74.00
TYLER, JULIA 2nd set, *First Ladies Series*, 1979-1981.....................125.00
TYROLEAN BOY & GIRL* 8" (20cm) hard plastic, bend knee walker, 1962-1965 ....198.00 each
  8" (20cm) hard plastic, bend knee, 1965-1972...............................155.00 each
  8" (20cm) straight legs, 1973...80.00 each

*Became Austria in 1974.

U.S.A. 8" (20cm) hard plastic, *International Dolls*, 1993-1994 ....$ 50.00
UNION OFFICER 12" (31cm) hard plastic/vinyl, *Scarlett Series*, 1990-1991 ....80.00
UNION SOLDIER 8" (20cm) hard plastic, *Scarlett Series*, 1991 ....85.00
UNITED STATES 8" (20cm) hard plastic, 1974-1975 ....75.00
  1976-1987 ....80.00
  1988-1992 ....50.00

VAN BUREN, ANGELICA 2nd set, *First Ladies Series*, 1979-1981 ....$ 125.00
VERMONT MAIDEN 8" (20cm) hard plastic, made for Enchanted Doll House, 1990 *(see Special Dolls)* 100.00

125

A dazzling pair of dolls are these 8in (20cm) *Romeo* and *Juliet* that were the 1994 mid-year release from the Alexander Doll Company. *A. Glenn Mandeville Collection.*

VICTORIA
21" (53cm) composition, 1939, 1941 ...$1,875.00 up
21" (53cm) composition, 1945-1946......1,850.00 up
14" (36cm) hard plastic, 1950-1951.........975.00
8" (20cm) hard plastic, matches 18" (46cm) doll, 1954..........975.00
18" (46cm) hard plastic, blue gown, *Me and My Shadow Series*, 1954................1,265.00

VICTORIA (BABY)
18" (46cm) cloth/vinyl, baby, 1966...........75.00
20" (51cm) cloth/vinyl, baby, 1967-1989....90.00
14" (36cm) cloth/vinyl, baby, 1975-1988, 1990-1994 ....95.00
20" (51cm) cloth/vinyl, baby, in dress, jacket, bonnet, 1986 ....95.00
14" (36cm) cloth/vinyl, baby, made for Lord & Taylor, 1989 *(see Special Dolls)* 95.00
18" (46cm) cloth/vinyl, baby, re-introduced, 1991-1993 ....85.00
VICTORIAN "so-called" 18" (46cm) hard plastic, pink taffeta and black velvet gown, *Glamour Girl Series*, 1953 ....1,300.00
VICTORIAN BRIDE 10" (25cm) hard plastic, *Portrette Series*, 1992....105.00
VICTORIAN SKATER 10" (25cm) hard plastic, *Portrette Series*, 1993-1994...100.00
VIETNAM 8" (20cm) hard plastic, 1968-1969................................285.00
1968-1969...300.00
8" (20cm) re-introduced in 1990-1991 ....55.00
VIOLET (Nutcracker Ballerina) 10" (25cm) *Portrette Series*, 1994 .....70.00
VIOLETTA 10" (25cm) hard plastic, 1987-1988.................................60.00

W

W.A.A.C. (ARMY) 14" (36cm) composition, 1943-1944...............$ 800.00
W.A.A.F. (AIR FORCE) 14" (36cm) composition, 1943-1944............800.00
W.A.V.E. (NAVY) 14" (36cm) composition, 1943-1944....................800.00
WALTZING 8" (20cm) hard plastic, 1955 ....655.00
WASHINGTON, MARTHA 1st set, *First Ladies Series*, 1976-1978 ....310.00
WELCOME HOME (DESERT STORM) 8" (20cm) hard plastic, boy or girl soldier, black or white, blonde or brunette, mid-year release 1991 ....55.00 up each

WENDY *(see Alexander-Kins)*
15" (38cm) hard plastic, 1955-1956 (Bride)..................................$ 500.00
18" (46cm) hard plastic, 1955-1956 (Bride)................................675.00
25" (64cm) hard plastic, 1955 (Bride) 925.00
8" (20cm) hard plastic, first MADC doll, MADC Doll Club, 1989
(see Special Dolls) 200.00
WENDY (FROM PETER PAN) 15" (38cm) hard plastic, 1953....................700.00
14" (36cm) plastic/vinyl, 1969...335.00
8" (20cm) hard plastic, slippers w/pom-poms, no faces,
Storyland Dolls, 1991-1994 ....55.00
WENDY ANGEL 8" (20cm) hard plastic, 1954..............................1,250.00
WENDY ANN *(see Alexander-Kins)*
9" (23cm) composition, painted eyes, 1936-1940 ....365.00
11-15" (28-38cm) composition, 1935-1948...................................560.00
14" (36cm) composition, in riding habit, 1938-1939 (some wigged) 450.00
17-21" (43-53cm) composition, 1938-1944 ....700.00-900.00
14-1/2–17" (37-43cm) hard plastic, 1948-1949.............................900.00
16-22" (41-56cm) hard plastic, 1948-1950................................900.00
23-25" (58-64cm) hard plastic, 1949 ....875.00
20" (51cm) hard plastic, 1956...565.00
WENDY HONORS THE MADAME 8" (20cm) hard plastic, mid-year
release, 1993 ....100.00
WENDY LOVES BEING A PROM QUEEN 8" (20cm) hard plastic, 1994............55.00
WENDY LOVES BEING BEST FRIENDS 8" (20cm) hard plastic,
MADC Doll Club *(see Special Dolls)* 125.00
WENDY LOVES BEING JUST LIKE MOMMY 1993-1994 ....75.00
WENDY LOVES BEING LOVED 8" (20cm) hard plastic doll and
wardrobe, gift box, mid-year release, 1992 ....105.00
WENDY LOVES Cherry Romper, 1994...25.00
Organdy Dress, 1994 ....20.00
WENDY LOVES HER ABC'S 8" (20cm) hard plastic, made for
ABC Unlimited Productions, 1993 *(see Special Dolls)* 85.00
WENDY LOVES HER FIRST DAY OF SCHOOL 8" (20cm) hard plastic, 1994 ....50.00
WENDY LOVES HER SUNDAY BEST 8" (20cm) hard plastic, 1994..................60.00
WENDY LOVES LEARNING TO SEW 8" (20cm) hard plastic,
Suitcase Sewing Kit, 1994 ....80.00
WENDY LOVES SUMMER 8" (20cm) hard plastic, box set, 1993-1994
(doll and wardrobe)...89.95
WENDY LOVES SUN DRESS 8" (20cm) hard plastic, 1993-1994 ....40.00
WENDY LOVES THE COUNTY FAIR 8" (20cm) hard plastic, 1993-1994............55.00
WENDY LOVES WINTER 8" (20cm) hard plastic, box set, 1994 ....90.00
WENDY SHOPS AT FAO 8" (20cm) hard plastic, made for
FAO Schwarz, 1993 *(see Special Dolls)*.....................................80.00
WENDY VISITS THE WORLD'S FAIR 1893 8" (20cm) made for
Shirley's Doll House, 1993 *(see Special Dolls)* 80.00
WHITE RABBIT cloth/felt, 1940s 550.00-650.00
WICKED WITCH OF THE WEST 8" (20cm) hard plastic, *Wizard of Oz
Series*, mid-year release, 1994...60.00
WILSON, EDITH 5th set, *First Ladies Series*, 1988....................................85.00

WILSON, ELLEN 5th set, *First Ladies Series*, 1988 ....$ 85.00
WINGED MONKEY 8" (20cm) hard plastic, *Wizard of Oz Series*, 1994...........50.00
WINNIE WALKER 15" (38cm) hard plastic, 1953 ....250.00
   18-23" (46-58cm)..400.00
   In trunk, trousseau, 1953-1954..900.00
WINTER 14" (36cm) plastic/vinyl, *Classic Dolls*, 1993 ....150.00
WINTER ANGEL 8" (20cm) factory altered doll for Shirley's Doll
   House, 1993 *(see Special Dolls)*..85.00
WINTER RAIN 14" (36cm) plastic/vinyl, *Classic Dolls*, 1994 ....120.00
WINTER SPORTS 8" (20cm) hard plastic, made for Shirley's Doll
   House, 1991 *(see Special Dolls)*..75.00
WINTER WONDERLAND 8" (20cm) hard plastic, made for Nashville
   Show, 1991 *(see Special Dolls)*..185.00
WINTER WONDERLAND II 8" (20cm) hard plastic, made for Nashville
   Show, 1992 *(see Special Dolls)*..95.00
WINTERTIME 8" (20cm) hard plastic, MADC Premiere, 1992
   (see Special Dolls) 195.00
WITCH 8" (20cm) hard plastic, *Americana Series*, 1992 ....55.00
   8" (20cm) hard plastic, *Americana Series*, 1992-1993.......................55.00
WITHERS, JANE 12-13–1/2" (31-34cm) composition,
   closed mouth, 1937...1,000.00
   15-17" (38-43cm), 1937-1939...1,250.00
   17" (43cm) cloth body,1939 ....1,350.00
   18-19" (46-48cm) 1937-1939...1,360.00
   19-20" (48-51cm) closed mouth version......................................1,450.00
   20-21" (51-53cm) 1937 ....1,850.00
WIZARD, THE 8" (20cm) hard plastic, *Wizard of Oz Series*,
   mid-year release, 1994..52.00
WOMEN IN THE GARDEN 10" (25cm) four dolls, one-of-a-kind
   Disney World® Auction, 1993 *(see Special Dolls)* 6,500.00
WYNKEN, BLYNKEN & NOD 8" (20cm) hard plastic, set of three
   dolls and a wooden shoe, *Storyland Dolls*, 1993-1994 ....200.00

Y

YOLANDA 12" (31cm) hard plastic/vinyl, slim teenage body,
   1965 (assorted outfits)...$ 345.00
YUGOSLAVIA 8" (20cm) hard plastic, bend knee, 1968-1972...............150.00
   8" (20cm) straight legs, 1973-1975 ....75.00
   8" (20cm) straight legs, 1976-1986 ....65.00
   8" (20cm) CU Gathering, 1987 FAD *(see Special Dolls)*..............150.00

Z

ZORINA BALLERINA 17" (43cm) composition, 1937-1938 ....$1,250.00